Holding Your Square

CRIME ETHNOGRAPHY SERIES

Series editors: Dick Hobbs and Geoffrey Pearson

Published titles

Holding Your Square: streetlife, masculinities and violence, by
Christopher W. Mullins

Narratives of Neglect: community, regeneration and the governance of security
by Jacqui Karn

Holding Your Square
Masculinities, streetlife and violence

Christopher W. Mullins

WILLAN
PUBLISHING

Published by

Willan Publishing
Culmcott House
Mill Street, Uffculme
Cullompton, Devon
EX15 3AT, UK
Tel: +44(0)1884 840337
Fax: +44(0)1884 840251
e-mail: info@willanpublishing.co.uk
website: www.willanpublishing.co.uk

Published simultaneously in the USA and Canada by

Willan Publishing
c/o ISBS, 920 NE 58th Ave, Suite 300
Portland, Oregon 97213-3786, USA
Tel: +001(0)503 287 3093
Fax: +001(0)503 280 8832
e-mail: info@isbs.com
website: www.isbs.com

Hardback
ISBN-13: 978-1-84392-194-3
ISBN-10: 1-84392-194-4

British Library Cataloguing-in-Publication Data

A catalogue record for this book is available from the British Library

Typeset by GCS, Leighton Buzzard, Beds
Project management by Deer Park Productions, Tavistock, Devon
Printed and bound by T.J. International, Padstow, Cornwall

For

Jerry A. Mullins
(1948–1992)

and

Jerry C. Mullins
(b. 1999)

who have taught me
the only things
I really needed to know
about masculinity.

Contents

Acknowledgements

Many people helped to make this project possible. I would like to specifically thank Richard Wright, Bruce Jacobs and Richard Rosenfeld for giving me access to their data for this project. Jody Miller, Scott Decker and Norman White also gave me access to their data sets, even though those data were eventually removed from the combined sample. Jody Miller deserves special thanks and commendation. During my tenure at UMSL, and especially during the process of completing the doctoral dissertation that served as the core of this volume, she was invaluable in giving freely of her time: to read my work, to chat, to encourage or anything else needed. Additionally, I owe a special debt of gratitude to Richard Wright, who has taken a strong interest in my career since we first met. Richard has gone out of his way to mentor and guide me and for that I am always grateful.

I would have got nowhere without the support of my family. My wonderful children, Jerry and Arwen, always greeted me with joy and love no matter how often I was gone, ignored them or was just generally stressed and grumpy. My love for them and their very presence motivated me more than they will ever know. Lastly, and most importantly, I must acknowledge the unwavering love and support of my wife, Robin. Her sacrifices have been without measure and I am always grateful for her truly being the better half of my life and my spirit. Without her, myself and everything I do would be truly lesser.

Foreword by Jody Miller

Christopher Mullins' *Holding Your Square* is a pathbreaking investigation. At its most basic level, it provides an important advance in criminological understandings of street violence. Feminist scholars have long argued that it is only with explicit attention to gender that crime can be fully understood and theorized. Yet in American criminology, gender too often is taken to mean women. Men, too, have experience, and are shaped by gender. Though criminologists deal disproportionately with the behaviors of men, this social fact is often taken for granted rather than theorized. Moreover, gender is routinely treated as nothing more than an individual-level attribute. In contrast, Mullins provides a rigorous, complex analysis of the structural and situational gendered underpinnings of men's violence. *Holding Your Square* provides compelling evidence that gender matters in the production and reproduction of street violence.

Mullins is by no means the first to argue that there are important linkages between masculinities and crime. He builds from the insights of scholars such as R. W. Connell, Michael Kimmel and James Messerschmidt, and rightly notes that early and contemporary subcultural theorists often speak about facets of masculinity construction without identifying these features as such. He also draws from the large body of feminist criminological theorizing that has examined the experiences of women in male-dominated criminal settings. Mullins demonstrates that important feminist insights can be gained by also investigating how men 'within such hierarchies obtain and maintain their empowered positions' (page 8).

Beyond these basic contributions, I draw the reader's attention to two especially notable facets of *Holding Your Square:* its unique methodological contribution, and the significant theoretical advances this work brings to the study of masculinities and crime. Mullins' methodological approach is distinct in several ways. His is one of the few criminological studies to utilize secondary qualitative data. This poses certain challenges, as Mullins discusses, but also comes with tremendous benefit. Primary data collection of any type, and perhaps especially for qualitative research, is a costly and time-consuming endeavor. Yet once the initial study is completed, there are rarely mechanisms in place to archive qualitative data for further and new analyses. *Holding Your Square* demonstrates the added scholarly value that can result. As qualitative research receives renewed appreciation within US criminology, my sincere hope is that we work together to develop a stronger collaborative network of scholars and create infrastructural supports for archiving and sharing qualitative datasets.

Mullins' study is not only based on secondary data, but specifically a merged dataset created by combining data from multiple investigations. Though each sample was drawn for different investigatory purposes (to study the enactment of drug robberies, retaliation, snitching, and carjacking), each dataset includes similarly criminally embedded individuals from the same community setting. Rather than a liability, the merged data are a distinct strength of Mullins' investigation: that he finds such strikingly common threads across studies is a testament to the powerful perceptual and situational influence of masculinities in offender street networks.

One additional methodological feature of *Holding Your Square* is noteworthy. A particular strength of qualitative analysis is its ability to illuminate the micro-level perceptual and interactional processes associated with crime, and to use these insights to develop and elaborate social theory. However, there remains a palpable divide within US criminology between positivist epistemologies (dominated by quantitative theory testing) and the interpretive epistemologies and inductive methods typically employed by qualitative scholars. Scholars in the former tradition are often skeptical of qualitative research. On the other hand, we have not necessarily advanced our cause to this audience, because our analysis procedures are rarely made sufficiently transparent to readers.

On this count, Mullins' work is exceptional: he provides a systematic description of his analysis techniques and the process of inductive theory development, and offers a thorough consideration of validity issues. *Holding Your Square* demonstrates that methodological rigor does not require a positivist orientation. Mullins' detailed attention to latent meanings, situational contexts (including the speech context of the interview), and his examination of nuance, contingency, and contradiction is a fine example of inductive theory development, and should serve as a model for future work in this area.

Finally, what theoretical insights do we gain from *Holding Your Square?* Many, I would offer. Most existing work on masculinities and crime has either been predominantly theoretical rather than empirical or has utilized small samples or case studies, and has 'focused on the broad contours of how masculinities shape offending' (page 44). Aided by the size and richness of his data, Mullins was able to explore multiple facets of masculinities and their operation on the streets. *Holding Your Square* examines what he refers to as four key experiential categories of gender, each of which is conceptualized as a structural force, situational concern, and perceptual preoccupation: doing gender, the accumulation of gender capital, the negotiation of gendered structures, and the nature of inter-gender interactions. In tracing the contours of street masculinities, Mullins' evidence is compelling that these are far from a full-scale rejection of the hegemonic forms of masculinity within mainstream US society. Instead, they are refracted through the limited opportunity structures found in isolated, disadvantaged minority communities and further distilled within streetlife culture.

Four facets of Mullins' analysis are of particular theoretical import: (1) the examination of hegemonic, counter-hegemonic, and subordinated masculinities on the streets, and the contested nature of these forms; (2) the illumination of the many situational nuances within masculinity challenges that make violent decision-making 'highly contingent on the immediate environment' (page 7); (3) the investigation of criminally embedded men's relations with and treatment of women; and (4) the emphasis on gendered role strains that emerge from the competing demands of practical and masculine reputational concerns.

Mullins' analysis of the dimensions of street masculinities demonstrates that 'gendered power on the streets is not as simple as men's dominance over women. Men vie with one another for prestige and street influence as well' (page 8), and this is a key constitutive site for violence. Key elements of hegemonic street masculinity appear to vary by age, and are influenced by the hegemonic forms found in mainstream society and the situational exigencies of streetlife. Existing works have noted the importance of independence, self-reliance, toughness, and fatalism, yet Mullins also demonstrates their nuances, contradictions, and interconnections. His analysis of the many facets of subordinated street masculinity – subsumed under the cognitive category 'punk' – is both fascinating and illuminating.

Likewise, while all women are subordinated within masculine street culture, Mullins' analysis reveals that men's relations with women, and the cognitive categories they place them in, are also multifaceted. Numerous studies have examined the contours of gender inequality in offender networks based on the experiences and perspectives of women. Yet there is also much to be learned by gaining insight into how and why – from their points of view – men exploit, discard, abuse, ignore, and protect the various women in their lives. Though Mullins notes that his data was admittedly thinnest in this arena – due to the research questions guiding the original investigations – he provides a fruitful analysis that raises important questions for future research.

Finally, Mullins' detailed analysis of the contradictions within street masculinities demonstrates one of the greatest strengths of well-executed qualitative research: its ability to illuminate the fissures and inconsistencies inherent in the value systems and behavioral demands associated with all structurally based, situationally constructed identities. *Holding Your Square* highlights the contingent nature of masculinity on the streets, yet demonstrates its penetrating influence in producing violence. In my view, it provides the most nuanced explication of the relationship between masculinities and crime yet produced in the US context.

Jody Miller
University of Missouri-St Louis

Chapter 1

Doing crime, doing gender

In a crowded bar, Red, a 43-year-old man, wove his way through the press of people. Accidentally, he stumbled and spilled his drink onto a man seated at the bar. Before Red could so much as offer up a 'sorry', the man spun around and slapped Red across the face, leaving a stinging handprint across his cheek. Humiliated, enraged, and feeling the eyes of everyone in the club on him, Red left the establishment. He went out to his car and retrieved his pistol; he sat in the car and waited. When he saw the man who slapped him exit the bar, Red crept through the shadowed parking lot, came up behind the man as he was unlocking his car and shot him seven times in the head.

While relaying the incident during an interview, Red showed no remorse for his action. Rather, he repeatedly emphasized that the man he killed was in the wrong. While he even characterized his own stumble as a 'mistake', in his recounting of the event Red insisted he would have made it 'right' by paying to have the man's shirt cleaned. But the victim never provided him with the opportunity. Red said that he 'felt bad' that he had been slapped in front of everyone in the tavern, that the man had made him 'look bad' in front of everyone. He claimed that 'a man don't never put his hand on another man, you know ... I ain't never in my life had a motherfucker smack me before'. He was compelled to respond and, in his mind, lethal violence was his only option.

How can we make sense of such seemingly senseless violence? Simply put, this violence is not senseless. As with all human behavior, it has a structure and logic. It is not the logic of a white, middle-class culture. Its causes and meanings are deeply rooted within a subculture of streetlife that thrives in our most disadvantaged communities. To understand these violences, we must understand the world in which its participants live, how they see their place within the culture of the streets and, most importantly, how they see themselves. All social life is guided by rules; all social actors draw upon these scripts when interacting with others. Red's description of his revenge-taking is no exception. Red's victim, at least in Red's account, broke the rules; he did not give Red a chance to apologize and provide restitution. He also violated the rules of masculinity in the way he struck Red: an open-hand smack across the face. That is the way one strikes a woman. A man deserves a punch – a sign of respect for his toughness. Thus, not only does Red have to repay the man's disrespect in general, he has to take back his own masculinity. The rules of street interaction definitely framed the homicide, and the events that precipitated it. Yet, inextricably fused with these scripts are the demands of masculinity. Red himself inserted the salience of gender into the episode in saying that *men* don't smack other *men*. On the streets, reputation is everything. Among deeply embedded, active street offenders, a key part of their reputations is the image of masculinity they convey.

In order to understand street violence, we must understand street masculinity, and vice versa. As sociologists who study gender have pointed out over the past few years, gender is not monolithic. There are multiple forms of both masculinities and femininities which vary depending upon their more immediate social context. Simply put, a middle-class male perceives and enacts masculinity differently from a criminally embedded lower-class male. The social and symbolic resources at their disposal are vastly different, as are the expectations of their peers.

This book is about how streetlife subcultures, especially gendered elements and demands with them, frame violence. By exploring the nature of streetlife, especially the forms of masculinities and femininities that exist within it, we can come to a more complete understanding of the role street violence plays in the lives and identities of subculture participants. Men on the streets do not just see violence as one of many potential tools at their disposal for navigating their daily lives and for enacting gender role demands. Many of these men, like Red, see it as an essential and central component of their selves and of the image they project to others. While even the most ruthless of these men are not always violent in every situation, they do draw on violence more frequently, and more severely, than is seen within our society more generally. It is my intent in this book to ask the question: 'Why?' The bulk of this first chapter will explore what prior researchers have discovered about streetlife subculture, about violence within those social networks and about the images and demands of gender that generate violent acts. It will also review the key theories of gender especially as it relates to crime in general and violence specifically.

Introduction

Criminologists have long been interested in the behavioral norms and values seen as unique to the streets. Since the mid-twentieth century, scholars have identified and explored a subculture that permeates criminal social networks. Such luminaries in the field as Walter Miller (1958) and Albert Cohen (1955) drew upon street-based field observations to define a core set of oppositional values held by those embedded within the life of the streets. Linking such beliefs and attitudes to the socio-economic status of the men and boys they interviewed, this work, along with that of Marvin Wolfgang and Franco Ferracuti (1967), became the core of the so-called 'subcultural' theories of crime and violence. Such interpretations argued that individuals within a lower-class community adopted attitudes toward violence that were a form of oppositional resistance to the behavioral demands of mainstream culture. These scholars saw crime etiologically as the product of an alternative set of values and attitudes held within a specific socio-economic location.

More recently, work done by the likes of Elijah Anderson (1990, 1999), Neal Shover (Shover 1996; Shover and Henderson 1995; Shover and Honaker 1992), and Richard Wright (Wright and Decker 1994, 1997) resurrected the notion of a street-based subculture. In such environments, social actors are driven by demands for instant gratification to engage in violent and property crime to rectify a 'pressing need for cash' to buy drugs and other status-enhancing items (see Shover and Henderson 1995; Shover and Honaker 1992; Wright and Decker 1994, 1997). More expressive instances of interpersonal violence derive from strongly held beliefs in the construction and defense of personal street reputation; violence is a tool for both the creation of and the defense of self-image (Anderson 1990, 1999). Compared with previous studies, these contemporary works illustrate that these are not holistic sets of attitudes held by members of lower-class communities, but reflect a set of marginal behavior patterns existing at the edges of these communities. Streetlife, as I use the term here, is a set of social structural behavioral demands that exist among individuals in an urban community who are deeply embedded in criminal activities and criminal social networks. Although this concept has its roots in Hagan and McCarthy's (1997) work on the criminal behavior of homeless adolescents in Canada, it has more direct connections to the work of Wright and Decker (1994, 1997) and Neal Shover (see Shover 1996; Shover and Henderson 1995; Shover and Honaker 1992). Drawn from interviews with both active and incarcerated offenders, this work clearly defines the sociocultural context in which criminal decision-making occurs. It highlights the deviant values and attitudes that form the core of these bounded thought processes and focuses attention on how streetlife behavioral demands shape crime's etiology.

All investigators who draw upon subcultural arguments have tied these values to men and their images of themselves. Oddly, none of these scholars have built on this obvious point to use existing strands of feminist theory to analyze these attitudes and accompanying behaviors as aspects of the gendered social structure of the streets. Theories built on subcultural approaches, especially recent advances, have focused on how the offender's perspective shapes motivation, target selection and enactment of street crime events. Such work has gone a long way to advance our understanding of these issues, but theoretical links to broader structural issues have typically focused only on issues related to de-industrialization. Gender as a structural force and situational concern is all but absent.

As the exploration of streetlife has experienced a resurgence within criminology, feminist criminology has begun to examine the experiences of women and men in streetlife contexts. Such work has brought structural models of gender to bear upon attitudes and behaviors within criminal social networks. Although work that links field data to feminist theories has been developed to explore women's criminality and streetlife experiences (see Maher 1997; Miller 2001), work involving men has remained largely theoretical. While there has been some rich ethnographic work along these lines in a British context (see Hobbs et al. 2003; Winlow 2001), James Messerschmidt's (1993, 1997, 2000, 2004) work is one of the few attempts within a US context. Through what he terms 'structured action theory', Messerschmidt theorizes that violence is a core component of masculinity. Crime in general and violence in particular provide a means to prove one's manhood in the eyes of one's self and one's peers.

This book unites these heretofore separate areas of inquiry, looking specifically at the forms that masculinities take within a social context and how these masculinities structure violent criminal action. It advances our understanding of street violence by incorporating feminist structural analysis with existing theories of streetlife's ties to crime. It also adds needed empirical investigation to existing theoretical work on the intersection of masculinity and crime. No study has yet systematically examined the relationship between masculinities and violence with a data set of the size and scope drawn upon here. By examining the intersection of broadly held gendered notions of self and social action with violent crime, this book aims to enhance our understanding of both streetlife and masculinities.

From here, the book presents a review of the literature on streetlife. Next, it examines the more theoretical discussions within feminist sociology and criminology on gender, with a particular emphasis on masculinity, before examining current trends in understanding the link between masculinities and criminal activity. Drawing from these works, I lay out the theoretical model for the current investigation, and close with an overview of the remainder of the study.

This book explores the interconnections of masculinities and violence on the streets of Saint Louis, Missouri. Its primary goal is to understand how definitions of masculinities within streetlife social networks shape men's perceptions and enactments of violence. Drawing upon secondary analysis of 110 interviews with active offenders, it explores the contours of masculinities on the streets of a Midwestern, rust-belt city, and how these gendered structures interact with and define the nature of street violence – both instrumental (e.g. robbery) and expressive (e.g. retaliatory vengeance).[1] It builds upon two existing but heretofore disconnected bodies within the criminological literature: work on the subculture of streetlife and work on masculinity and crime. Through an exploration of how men define their own gendered self-concepts and their gendered perceptions of their street peers, this book examines how street-based gender identity motivates men toward and guides them through violent encounters. This relationship is reciprocal: the ever-present threat of violence also shapes the nature of masculinities.

Theorizing masculinity

Diverse theoretical approaches have evolved in recent decades to explain the role of gender in social life and the links between gender and crime. Early work in sociology conceived of gender and gendered behaviors as products of fixed sex roles – rigid behavioral expectations growing out of essentialized sex difference (see Roy 2001, esp. Chapters 1 and 5). Men and women were defined as different in both physiological and psychological constitution. Through recourse to social scientific (see Freud 1924; Parsons 1955) and popular discourses, differences in social action between the genders were attributed to these perceived innate differences. This early sociological work later evolved to form the basis of a sex role theory that attributed these differences not to innate qualities, but to socialization into ascribed roles continually seen as dichotomous. Masculinity and femininity were defined in relation to and in opposition with one another. With this rigid approach, gender was conceptualized as two separate but static role demands. Save for some attempts to explain the 'exceptional' nature of female crime (e.g. Pollak 1950), criminologists did not bring gender to bear in etiological studies of crime. It was taken for granted that crime was a male endeavor.

Over the past decades, the study of gender in a variety of disciplines has begun to take the exploration and theorization of masculinities seriously. As conceptualizations of gender became increasingly processual, dynamic and dialectical, feminist scholars realized that a full accounting of gender and gendered lives entailed not only an examination of men's lives, in addition to the growing scholarship on women's experiences, but a more complex envisioning of male experiences and worldviews beyond representing men as simple animus to women.

Masculinity scholars began to suggest there was a wide diversity among men in their experiences and enactments of power. Paralleling the growing focus on issues of intersectionality in women's lived experiences and social positions, it became clear that men in a variety of social positions engage masculinities in a plurality of fashions. Such theoretical insights have been slower to penetrate criminological inquiry.

Gender, structure and action

As with any major aspect of social structure, gender pervades all realms of action and organization within most social systems. It is indeed potentially omnirelevant to any social interaction (West and Zimmerman 1987). Connell (2002) has offered the most exhaustive detailing of how gender shapes action, perception and thought at all levels of analysis. To ascertain the influences of gender, one must identify and theorize its operation at the macro (gender order), meso (gender regime) and micro levels (gender relations). At the level of gender order, we find the systematic establishment of privilege and disadvantage across institutional environments. It is also the terrain of cultural images and expectations. Yet, we must not assume that these patterns are fixed and ahistorical; rather, they are contingent and in frequent flux.

Gender regimes pattern gendered interactions within organizations, institutions and networks. How one accomplishes (or rejects) gender varies between social locations. Expectations within families may differ strongly from those of the workplace, the classroom, or the nightclub. While these gender regimes are tied into patterns exhibited within the gender order, the precise contours and meanings will be highly contingent upon the immediate environment.

Gender relations consist of the face-to-face interactions that fill social actors' daily lives. It is the location of the enactment of the forces that prevail at the macro and meso levels, it is also the specific site of the reproduction of these forces. Much work at this level of analysis has drawn heavily upon interactionist frameworks emphasizing the situational accomplishment of gender; this approach is typically referred to as 'doing gender'. Building upon the work of Garfinkel (1967) and Goffman (1983, 1955, 1959), West and Zimmerman (1987: 127) assert that 'participants in interaction organize their various and manifold activities to reflect or express gender, and they are disposed to perceive the behavior of others in a similar light'. The process of actualizing normative gender expectations – commonly called 'doing gender' – guides the ways that behavioral decisions are made, self-presentations are constructed and others' actions are predicted and interpreted. Social actors engage and reproduce gendered structures in their daily, mundane behaviors (West and Fenstermaker 1995; West and Zimmerman 1987). With this conceptual approach, gender is 'much more than a role or an individual characteristic: it is a mechanism whereby situated social action contributes to the reproduction of social structure' (West and Fenstermaker 1995: 21). Social action is the scaffolding of social structure; it is through the enactment of gendered behavioral demands that gendered social structure is reproduced within every social interaction. This approach implies that gender is 'potentially omnirelevant' (West and Fenstermaker 1995: 18) to all actions and activities.

A key element of 'doing gender' is what Goffman (1955, 1983) identified as presenting 'face' – the 'image of self delineated in terms of approved social attributes' (1955: 5). Social actors present images that are consistent with internalized self-concept and externally consistent with social expectations. When these projected images fail, an actor is 'out of face' or 'in wrong face'. When such an instance occurs, the actor must respond by adjusting his or her 'line' – the pattern of 'verbal and non-verbal acts' (1955:5) presented within a social situation – to regain face. Gender is a crucial area for the maintenance of face and exerts strong influence on what constitutes an acceptable line.

Such a dynamic presentation of self, especially a gendered self, highlights the agency that social actors bring to interactions. Recognizing that normative demands and organizational relationships may constrain social behavior, 'doing gender' emphasizes the ways individuals actively engage, reproduce and sometimes redefine gender in the course of social interaction. For instance, feminist ethnography emphasizes that while gendered social structures have a powerful effect on identity and behavior, individuals work through these structural constraints in a highly nuanced fashion (see Maher 1997; Miller 1998; Montgomery 2001). Social structures open some opportunities for social action while closing others, and individuals cogently navigate the social landscapes where they live (Maher 1997).

In criminology, most feminist ethnography has examined these issues in the context of female criminality. The approach is also useful as a framework for examining male offending. The exploration of how offenders negotiate gendered structures has been directed toward understanding how disempowered or marginalized social actors, such as women, manage to accomplish their goals within a power hierarchy. It is similarly useful to explore how dominant individuals within such hierarchies obtain and maintain their empowered positions. Gendered power on the streets is not as simple as men's dominance over women; men vie with one another for prestige and street influence as well. They must navigate their presentation of self for other men in the context of streetlife in order to establish, maintain, and extend their reputations. If, as previous research suggests, masculinity is central to the identity of men embedded in streetlife, how they interpret their actions – not just to others, but to themselves – will also be affected by such negotiation processes. Contemporary sociological work on gender emphasizes a concern with agency and dynamic social processes. In addition, as discussed below, recent work has also broadened our understanding of gender beyond the notion of two monolithic and oppositional gender categories.

Hegemonic masculinities

The central work of R. W. Connell (1987, 1993, 1995, 2002) changed the way sociologists theorize and study masculinity. Connell was the first to emphasize that multiple masculinities and femininities are possible within a given social setting. Moreover, these masculinities and femininities, defined as sets of gendered behavioral expectations, come with varying degrees of reward or censure. For instance, the primary set of gendered expectations held within mainstream culture, such as the male breadwinner role and the female mothering role, tend to be rewarded. Others, such as a stay-at-home father or childless woman, are subordinate; they are gendered performances that are less valued, and often defined as deviant.

Despite the varieties of gendered performances available to social actors, in western society masculinity has a hegemonic (Gramsci 1992) quality that cuts across other social structures. According to Connell (1987: 183), hegemonic masculinity, the socially constructed set of behavioral expectations that exerts its influence on all men in a society, is 'constructed in relation to various subordinated masculinities as well as in relation to women'. In addition to their relational nature, masculinities are also processual, because they are 'simultaneously a place in gender relations, the practices through which men and women engage that place, and the effects of these practices in bodily experience, personality and culture' (Connell 1995: 71). Through historical change, social position and individual interpretation, numerous masculinities are constructed and implemented in proximate social spaces (see also Connell and Messerschmidt 2005). This emphasis on situationality is crucial. All social action is simultaneously 'situational ... and transformative' (Connell 1993: 602). It is impossible to enact any set of socially acquired behavioral expectations and not through that process alter their own foundational aspects. Social enactment reproduces, modifies, intensifies, de-emphasizes, refracts and/or rearranges the original normative constellations.

At its core, hegemonic masculinity is based upon the legitimation of gender definitions that require the subordination of women to men and the subordination of non-hegemonic masculinities (for example, 'sissies' or 'punks') to the dominant form. For men, these definitions shape larger gender performances by enforcing a set of acceptable scripts through which they can establish and 'prove' their masculinity. Men constantly face the need to reinforce their masculine status as it is constantly policed by their peers (Connell

1993, 1995, 2002; Connell and Messerschmidt 2005). Likewise, the definitions create a set of scripts that simultaneously direct and reward female role performances toward acceptable femininities (e.g. maternal care giving) and sanction those performances that are less valued or deviant (for example, lesbian or empowered femininities). Specifically, hegemonic masculinity generates what Connell refers to as an 'emphasized' femininity that is focused on 'accommodating the interests and desires of men' (Connell 1987: 183). This emphasized femininity restricts women to subordinate social statuses in both public and domestic social spaces. Male gatekeepers restrict women's legitimate and illegitimate opportunities for material acquisition and enforce behavioral expectations of submissiveness to and compliance with masculinist demands. Thus, hegemonic masculinity defines both appropriate male and female social action, shapes the way social actors perceive their own and others' behavior, and frames the ways that men view and interact with both women and men.

Of essential import for this study is the realization that hegemonic masculinity, and its dialectically intertwined mates – subordinate masculinities and emphasized femininities – vary by social location. Thus, this constellation of gendered features necessitates empirical examination at three levels: local, regional and global (Connell and Messerschmidt 2005: 849). Global hegemonic masculinities are those that are currently emerging within international and transnational institutions and contexts (see also Kimmel 2005). These forces will apply pressure to both regional and global structures in direct and indirect ways (for example, see Hobbs *et al.* 2003 and Winlow 2001 for an exploration of how post-industrial forces transformed working-class masculinities in the UK). Regional refers to those gendered structures at the level of nation-state and culture, what is typically referred to as the macro-level in sociological work. Finally, the local level combines both face-to-face locations of social interaction and the broader meso-level gender regimes that encapsulate those interactions. This study will devote itself to the description and analysis of masculinities within streetlife criminal subculture – a highly specific socio-historical location. Thus, with the need to firmly and thoroughly establish gender regime and the contours of gender relations, it is necessary to turn towards the discussion of the nature of life within criminal subcultures within the US. From there, I proceed to elucidate how gender operates within that environment.

Streetlife

Criminology has long realized that street crime and violence tends to be strongly localized in specific social environments. Interpersonal violence, while occurring across most social divides, has been, in the modern era, strongly correlated with specific social conditions. While theoretical explanations of these patternings have proliferated, the fact that certain places exhibit higher levels of violence and crime than others remains. One thread of research and theory has suggested that due to a combination of social dislocation and distance, impoverished communities may develop a set of subcultural values and behavioral expectations that run counter to (or at least deviate from) mainstream demands. In postulating a subculture tied to criminal behavior, these theories provide a lens for understanding the integration of criminality into daily life. Before this book turns to an exploration of how gender moulds streetlife behavioral expectation, it first explores the development of these theories, then discusses the current state of the field.

The 'discovery' of streetlife

Once US criminology took a sociological turn away from biological or trait theories of crime, and toward structural (e.g. Merton 1938) and socialization (e.g. Sutherland 1939) approaches, fieldwork began to produce a body of research that identified subcultural values as a key cause of crime and criminality. This early work tended to claim that such values and attitudes were ubiquitous among residents of lower-class neighborhoods and overemphasized a concentration of street crime in these communities. These aspects have been critiqued over the years, but the basic findings remain pertinent.

Cohen (1955) produced the first subcultural theory of crime[2] in his book *Delinquent Boys*, in which he critiqued the economic aspects of Merton's (1938) Anomie Theory. Instead, Cohen focused on what he saw as a subculture of resistance among adolescents raised in lower-class communities. He did not, however, entirely reject Merton's notion of anomie and strain, but localized its primary effect in the experiences that lower-class boys had in school. Claiming that schools held all students to a 'middle-class measuring rod' of behavior that emphasized such values as delayed gratification, hard work, and courtesy toward one's superiors, Cohen argued that boys raised in the absence of these values were likely to fail in their execution. They experienced 'status frustration' because of their inability to enact middle-class values. In response to this frustration, a set of values resistant to those of the middle class developed and was adopted by some boys in these communities, especially those who joined street gangs. This subculture was characterized by hedonism, impulsivity and maliciousness, which were transformed into criminal behavior as a way to resist marginalization.[3] Cohen was clear that this represented only one possible response to status frustration, and he offered this as the dominant explanation for crime within these communities.

Following Cohen, Walter Miller (1958) published an influential article that defined what he called the 'focal concerns' of lower-class culture, expressed in the behavior and attitudes of lower-class juveniles. These scripts still read as a checklist for masculinity enactment: toughness (physical and mental), avoiding trouble, smartness (quick-wittedness and the value of street smarts over academic learning), the search for excitement, an overpowering sense of fatalism, and a strong desire to maintain autonomy from others. Miller explained delinquency as a natural enactment of these subcultural values. Fighting, theft, drug and alcohol use, and illegal gambling were all ways that youths manifested these concerns. The constant drive for excitement and the overpowering sense of fate further reinforced criminal activities among youth embedded in streetlife.

Building upon the idea that subcultural values and attitudes caused crime in certain lower-class locations, Wolfgang and Ferracuti (1967) argued that poor urban neighborhoods were the location of a subculture of violence. This set of values and attitudes emphasized the need to physically respond to challenges against a man's personal honor. Wolfgang and Ferracuti argued that such values were learned by boys during childhood socialization, and were then passed down from generation to generation. This acceptance of violence was also seen in other social situations, such as the use of severe physical punishment in disciplining children and in domestic disputes.

This work has generated several criticisms. One of the strongest is that broader survey-based measures failed to show that lower-class people hold significantly different attitudes from the rest of society (e.g. Sampson and Bartusch 1999). Such work questions whether a unified set of deviant subcultural values dominates an entire class stratum. Others have criticized subcultural explanations on the grounds that delinquency is not isolated within the lower classes (Hirschi 1969), and that middle-class boys also display some of the same values and attitudes identified as causes of violence and crime (Cernkovich 1978). Additionally, this work has been criticized for ignoring female crime or for simply ascribing it to attachments to delinquent boys and men (Chesney-Lind 1997; Maher 1997). These critiques, the emergence of control theories, and the resurgence of rational-choice models, helped criminology drift away from subcultural models of violence. This book is focused on men and masculinities, so the well-reasoned critiques concerning the explanations of female crime are not directly relevant. Recent work has addressed issues concerning the pervasiveness of these values throughout American culture and their prevalence within lower-class communities, and this discussion now turns in that direction.

The code of the street and the culture of desperate partying

In recent decades, some sociologists and criminologists have returned to fieldwork and to subcultural explanations of violence and crime. Current work does not claim that all lower-class communities hold strongly oppositional values. Rather, this work has identified a marginal subculture existing within these communities, where only a small portion of the residents internalize and activate its demands. It is within those social networks that both crime and the subculture of streetlife exist. Self-report studies, especially longitudinal ones, indicate that a small number of people tend to commit most offenses, especially serious offenses (Visher 2000). A study of males in Philadelphia who were born in 1945 found that 18 per cent of the sample was responsible for 52 per cent of the reported crime in the sample (Wolfgang, Figlio and Sellin 1972). Similarly, a study of a cohort of males born in Racine, Wisconsin in 1955 found that 6.5 per cent of the sample was responsible for 70 per cent of all felony crimes reported (Shannon 1988).

The resurrection of criminological interest in streetlife coincided with a decline of urban centers within the US due to global forces of de-industrialization and the general shift toward the post-industrial era. Predominantly minority, inner-city neighborhoods experienced significant losses of jobs, which had wide-reaching effects on almost all social institutions within these communities. Crime rates increased, as did the frequency of family fractures, the poverty rate and the unemployment rate. This in turn led to a loss of tax income in urban areas which often translated into poor public services – including police protection and reduced school quality. Combined with a loss of general community collective efficacy, these trends began to spiral in on themselves, creating a feedback loop of disadvantage that was worsened by the general conservative turn in the funding of social service programs seen under the administration of Ronald Reagan during the 1980s (see Wilson 1987, 1996). It is within this context that criminologists began exploring criminal subcultures within these urban locales.

Elijah Anderson's work (1990, 1999) highlights this concentration of criminality within a small population. Drawing upon fieldwork in Philadelphia, he identifies two broad value orientations in the Germantown neighborhood: 'decent' and 'street' families. The former embrace more typical working-class values and behavior norms, while the latter reject mainstream values and norms in their embrace of the 'code of the street', a code that emphasizes maintaining one's personal reputation at all costs and above all other social concerns. According to Anderson, this code arose through a combination of (1) the lack of living wage jobs caused by de-industrialization; (2) historical and contemporary racial discrimination; (3) the collapse of public services; (4) the effects of the crack cocaine epidemic; and (5) a profound sense of alienation resulting from these structural problems. Interpersonal violence and adherence to the principles of a flashy street fashion sense form the core of self-presentation on the streets. Potential and actual violence become central concerns as the primary methods used to establish 'juice' on the streets.

Anderson ascribes the continued existence of the code to the perception among 'street' families that 'little that is conventional retains legitimacy. The most desperate people … become mired in an outlaw culture … that … becomes legitimate to its adherents because the wider system … has little legitimacy' (1999: 320). Thus the code gains a life of its own and reproduces within communities of concentrated disadvantage. Because these behaviors occur in public space – literally on the streets – they create the impression in communities external to these neighborhoods of being the modal form of behavior of all lower-class community residents. While Anderson's work refutes this claim, he nonetheless notes that even those who do not internalize the 'code' must be familiar with it and live by its rules when moving through the geographies it dominates. Simply, if individuals must travel to the corner to catch a bus or buy a carton of milk, they must know the behavioral norms of the 'code'.

Throughout his work, Anderson emphasizes that at its core this is a code of masculinity. Constructions of manhood on the streets generate the focus on respect, and the reversion to violence when it is questioned[4] (see Anderson 1999: 91–93). He further ties the code to other expressions of masculinity, including the display of heterosexual prowess gained via sexual conquest (see specifically Anderson 1990: Chapter 4; Anderson 1999: Chapter 4). Men's inability to enact mainstream masculine breadwinning roles is also tied to their involvement in the drug economy and avoidance of marriage (Anderson 1999: Chapters 3 and 5). He clearly situates much of the code as a set of alternative prestige structures that men activate in the absence of historically available working-class masculinities, but Anderson fails to fully articulate the gendered nature of these perceptions and demands.

Richard Wright and Scott Decker conducted two pivotal studies in Saint Louis, Missouri, that analyzed large samples of active burglars (1994) and armed robbers (1997). Although their work emphasizes issues of target selection, enactment and goods disposal, their analysis of offender motivation locates active offenders in the context of what Shover and Honaker (1992: 283) call street culture: a set of values and attitudes that stress the experience of 'good times with minimal concern for obligations and commitments that are external' to these demands. In both their studies, Wright and Decker (1994, 1997) emphasize that crime is motivated by a pressing need for cash to 'keep the party going'. This typically involves the purchase of drugs and alcohol, but also entails spending freely on expensive, fashionable clothing and other status items. Increased status may enhance their ability to fulfill their desires for sexual conquest (see also Anderson 1990, 1999).

The desire for spontaneity, demands for instant gratification, and the rejection of legitimate work as both 'boring' and impinging on their independence, exert pressure on men to engage in acquisitive crimes (see also Akerstrom 1985; Irwin 1980; Tunnell 1992, 2000). Robbery and burglary provide an immediate source of resources, allow for the maintenance of independence and provide a sensual thrill that offsets the mundane nature of everyday life (see also Katz 1988). Thus, according to Wright and Decker, streetlife and crime are woven together in a mutually reinforcing fashion.

These more recent studies offer continued support for the earlier findings of the subculture school. Instead of suggesting that streetlife is a set of attitudes common to all individuals in a lower-class neighborhood, however, this work indicates that only a small minority of community residents engages in these behaviors. Despite the small number of adherents, this set of demands is believed responsible for a large portion of the street crime found within disadvantaged communities. The demands of street-corner society generate drug sales and purchases, prostitution, burglary, petty theft, armed robbery, carjacking, and high levels of interpersonal violence (Jacobs 2000; Shover 1996; Shover and Henderson 1995; Shover and Honaker 1992; Wright and Decker 1994, 1997). As with the earlier work, recent research also indicates that these social networks are strongly dominated by men (see also Steffensmeier 1983; Steffensmeier and Terry 1986). Most of the demands of streetlife are not merely focused on successful criminality but on maintaining one's image as a *man* on the streets.

Masculinities, subculture and crime

As noted above, little work has explicitly examined the relationship between masculinities and crime. Messerschmidt (1993, 1997, 2000, 2004), in what he terms 'structured action theory', unites the two trends in feminist sociology discussed above in order to address this limitation. In his model, two elements are crucial for understanding the linkages between gender and crime. First, drawing from the concepts of 'doing gender', Messerschmidt argues that social structure and social action are reciprocal: 'Social structures are realized only through social action and social action requires structure as its condition' (1997: 113). Second, drawing from Connell's (1995) work on masculinities, Messerschmidt emphasizes that the role demands of masculinity will vary within a given social structure and in any given situation. These theoretical postulates are united to explore the linkages between masculinities and crime.

According to Messerschmidt, 'men situationally accomplish masculinity in response to their social structured circumstances ... [V]arious forms of crime can serve as suitable resources for doing masculinity within the specific social context of the street'[5] (1993: 119). Especially in the absence of more normative and mainstream avenues to masculinity construction (e.g. work and family life), criminal action of any sort can be used to exhibit masculine traits such as courage, toughness and the willingness to take risks. The generation of masculinity via offending arises out of a key masculinity that Kimmel (1996: 17) places at the heart of United States culture: the self-made man. Since the nation's inception, he argues, the key forces shaping hegemonic masculinity in the United States have been those that focus on an individual's need to exhibit levels of socially prescribed success through individual action, primarily 'activities in the public sphere, measured by accumulated wealth and status'. Especially in social environments where mainstream social and cultural capitals are less available, Collison (1996: 440) notes, 'a masculine self identify [is] fashioned around money, consumption, toughness and respect'. Additionally, if the crime is acquisitive in nature (e.g. robbery, theft, pimping) those illicit proceeds can then be used for conspicuous consumption, which assists in the construction of many situated masculinities. According to Messerschmidt, if more acceptable sources of masculine capital are not available, men in certain social situations will view crime as a 'masculine-validating resource' (Messerschmidt 1993: 83).

Violence, specifically, has been identified as an acceptable avenue to accomplish masculinity (see Adler and Polk 1996; Graham and Wells 2003; Hobbs 1994; Hobbs *et al.* 2003; Mullins, Wright and Jacobs 2004; Polk 1994; Sim 1994; Tomsen 1997; Winlow 2001). Additionally, those who have successfully used violence in this manner should be inclined to continue doing so. Messerschmidt (2000) suggests that violence is most likely to occur when a man or boy is directly confronted with an affront to his masculinity. These 'masculinity challenges' present a distinct threat to a man's position. A violent response not only resolves the threat, but also re-establishes the challenged man's masculine capital or identity. In a recent study of homicides, for example, Polk (1994) analyzed how masculinity guided social actors within these events: public challenges between men produced violent events that often turned lethal. Adler and Polk (1996) uncovered similar processes within child homicide cases, wherein motivation often emerged from the man's authority or power having been challenged in some fashion.

Through the ethnographic study of bouncers in multiple cities, British scholars have also recently contributed a body of work that strongly connects a specifically situated masculinity and violence as action and capital (see Hobbs *et al.* 2003; Winlow 2001). Grounding their work in the transition of the UK's economy into a post-industrial realm where many urban centers rely more and more upon night-time leisure pursuits for economic health and well-being, this body of work specifically examines how bouncing has become one of the few outlets for working-class men to actualize a masculine sense of self rooted in the enactment of violence – both potential and actual. With the loss of more traditional industrial job opportunities, young working-class men sought new avenues for establishing their masculinity in the eyes of themselves and others. Street and pub fights had long stood as one way to do so. Bouncing combines an opportunity to earn money by cashing in on masculine capital earned through toughness exhibited via street fights.

Similar processes of socio-economic transition have occurred within the United States and have also strongly reshaped the contours of life within the working and lower classes, especially within communities dominated by racial minorities (see Wilson 1987, 1995). Some recent qualitative work has identified the role that violence increasingly plays within these communities, especially within the lives of young (and not-so-young) men. While not grounded in feminist-influenced frameworks, Anderson (1990, 1999) and Katz (1988) both explore how violent presentations of self become ways for young men, especially in disadvantaged (economically, ethnically, or racially) communities, to display and prove masculinity to their peers. The presentation of toughness, or the image of oneself as a 'badass', is not only manifest in symbolic manners of dress and self-presentation, but also in violent activities such as fighting. Such violence, despite its highly symbolic character, can be seen as instrumental in its goals in that it is directed toward the production of gendered capital – resources that are used to establish masculinity on the streets (Campbell 1999).

Due to an emphasis on control, individuality and toughness, men test other men in playful and serious contests to establish street credibility and masculine currency (Anderson 1990, 1999). This testing has a strongly public nature, being done within and in front of peer groups. Such a social display is essential to generate the capital sought from the activity. Violence researchers have shown that assaults are more likely to be fatal in the company of peers (see Riedel and Welsh 2002), whose presence seems to spur combatants on to more serious (and more lethal) violence. The peer context is an essential element here as it is other men in the social situation that award or remove masculine capital based on the social actor's behavior.

Interpreting criminal behavior through the lens of gendered structured action has proven theoretically and empirically valuable. Messerschmidt's work (1993, 1997, 2000) emphasizes how behavioral demands of street masculinity, which emphasize toughness, independence and the elevation of one's position through the devaluation of others, contribute to men's use of violence. He postulates that men use violence to establish and maintain an image of themselves as men – in their own eyes and the eyes of others. Likewise, Anderson's work (1990, 1999) has identified how masculinities, situated and structured by the code of the streets, guide if not compel some African-American men into violent interactions. Anderson's work highlights the relationship between offending and victimization, with the code of the streets establishing techniques of self-presentation that simultaneously emphasize ways to avoid victimization and to respond to victimization when it occurs.

Much work indicates the existence of criminal subcultures, especially within lower-class communities, that connect expectations of violence to expectations of masculinity (Anderson 1990, 1999; Bourgois 1996; Cohen 1955; Collier 1998; Collison 1996; Hobbs *et al.* 2003; MacLeod 1995; Miller 1958; Willis 1977; Winlow 2001). This body of work suggests that due to a lack of access to mainstream resources for masculinity construction, alternative means of acquiring masculine capital arise. Theorizing these behaviors as not only masculine, but as a form of situated masculinity tied to lower socio-economic class environments is not new, and, as noted above, has been met with serious critique. Violence and other crime also seem to serve as ways for middle-class youth to obtain masculine capital (Messerschmidt 2000); so what is unique about street culture?

This raises specific concerns about how well masculinity, as a set of behavioral demands, can explain men's use of violence. Indeed, qualitative (and quantitative) investigation needs to specify the intervening factors that generate the use of violence as a means of masculinity construction. This is especially necessary if we are to avoid tautological pitfalls. To simply assert that violence is a way for men to 'do gender' or construct a masculine identity is of no theoretical import for understanding the etiological connections between masculinity and crime, and often obscures more than it illuminates (see Miller 2002). Instead, empirical research must specify whether, when and how gender matters in the enactment of violence. To this end, the analysis that follows focuses on examining the role of gender in shaping criminal behavior on the streets. The analysis investigates four key experiential categories in which research suggests gender matters: doing gender, the accumulation of gender capital, the negotiation of gendered structures, and the nature of inter-gender interactions within criminal and non-criminal social networks.

Theoretical foci

This study seeks to unite the above discussed and heretofore disparate fields of inquiry within criminology. As the analysis unfolds, its direction will be the exploration of how gendered issues and concerns structure streetlife subcultural networks.

Doing gender

As explored above, the linkage of masculinity and crime is deep within the criminological literature. Work on streetlife connects the accomplishment of crime to presentation of self – especially masculine presentation of self. Crime is seen, in part, as a path for masculinity construction in the absence of otherwise legitimate means for its accomplishment. Here, 'doing gender' refers to the engagement in violence in order to establish masculine capital – violence used as a resource to prove masculinity to one's peers and associates. Thus, a relevant facet of the inquiry here is to examine men's descriptions of violent incidents – as witnesses, participants, and in their general discourse on how, when, and why to resolve an encounter violently. In this way we can ascertain the extent to which their discussions make reference to masculinity.

As mentioned above, men who successfully use violence in street interactions should be likely to do so again in the future. Prior work suggests that men draw upon their own successful violent performances to define themselves in their own eyes as *real* men and to gauge their own future violent behavior. Once they have proven themselves as capable of 'doing gender' in this way, it should become a resource for future gender performances. If this is so, men should carefully observe how other men respond to slights and violent challenges on the streets; their cognitive maps should include judgments of the masculinity of other men they interact with – not just in general but also in direct comparison to themselves. This would allow them not only to judge themselves in reference to others, but also to keep track of potential targets for expressive or instrumental violence in the future. Anderson (1999) points out that men are constantly testing each other on the streets; men who fail challenges are marked as potential targets in the future, while success prevents future challenges. To explore these dynamics, close attention in the analysis focuses on the reasons men give for selecting targets, their descriptions of other men's responses to violent victimization, and violence and how they frame their own responses to victimization. Critical for this project is the extent to which masculinity emerges as meaningful in the discussions, descriptions, resolutions and justifications of these challenges.

Accumulation of gender capital

Miller (2002) and Collison (1996) point out that a given behavior may not immediately be directed toward 'doing gender', but can precede gender construction activities. Acquisitive crimes of various forms (e.g. armed robbery, burglary, carjacking) are activities in which the primary goal of the action may not be the immediate construction of gender. Rather, they help men accumulate resources that will then play a role in future gendered presentations of self. As Wright and Decker (1994, 1996) have shown, many men use the proceeds from their crimes to build masculine street credibility via the purchase of drugs, cars, clothes, and pursuit of sexual conquest. In fact, they highlight this 'keeping up of appearances' as one of the key uses of illicit funds gained from crime (in addition to the purchase of drugs and alcohol). However, in that work, these activities are not examined to see if they are directly antecedent to masculinity construction. Although there are other rewards to this sort of behavior, the establishment and enhancement of an image on the streets as a *real* man may be more central to why these appearances need to be maintained. Thus, I examine men's explanations of how these resources are spent and the discussions they provide, to find out whether and how criminal proceeds are used to construct a masculine presentation of self.

Previous research suggests that spreading knowledge of one's violent actions can also serve as a way to facilitate future gender performances. Knowledge of prior violence enhances others' perceptions of the actor as violent, and thus masculine (e.g. Katz 1988). Reputation by itself may serve as a form of masculine capital during social interactions; it is a resource to be spent in establishing how one man relates to another in the power hierarchy of the streets. However, if too many specifics are widely known, this can provide ample opportunity for wronged parties to take violent revenge (Topalli, Wright and Fornango 2002) or for snitches to provide information to the police (see Rosenfeld, Jacobs and Wright 2003). These oppositional goals might create variation among men in regard to how this is navigated. To sort out these oppositional forces, this book will examine whether and how men balance their attempts to develop a street reputation as a dangerous 'badass' while at the same time avoid their activities being too broadly known.

The negotiation of gendered structures

Previous work suggests that structural elements of gender demands frame behaviors in such a fashion that a social actor will draw upon gender norms and gendered expectations in the accomplishment of criminal actions. However, the accomplishment of criminal action may entail surmounting or avoiding gendered obstacles. These impediments operate within the organization of social networks and social groups. While many of these activities involve playing upon gender norms, they are significant in their manipulation of structurally imposed and seated inequalities. Among women, the use of sexual availability in target selection is a clear example. 'Viccing', as Maher terms it, involves women playing upon masculinist expectations of female behavior in order to victimize men. At its root, viccing is the exploitation of men's socially constructed blind spots toward females' potential criminal motivations and activities (see also Katz 1988). Such behavior allows women to navigate the gendered perceptions of their victims (Miller 1998), escape the limitations imposed on them by their co-offenders (Mullins and Wright 2003), and avoid suspicion by the police (Jacobs and Miller 1998).

As discussed above, while developed in the understanding of female criminality, this issue may also be useful to understand how men negotiate street-based power hierarchies. If previous work on masculinity is correct, men should have to avoid being devalued by others and simultaneously establish themselves as superior. While many of women's gender negotiations focus on 'getting by' in a sexist streetlife network, men's negotiations should be about establishing dominance and control, not only over women but over other men as well. Analysis here explores whether, when and how men's violence and narratives of violence are framed within these processes of hierarchy negotiation.

Inter-gender interactions

The streets are strongly gender segregated. Men and women do not interact with great frequency in this social location. When they do, it is often on terms that the men establish. Research has found that men tend to view women as objects for the fulfillment of their personal desires and objectives, rather than as equals (Maher 1997; Miller 2001; Mullins and Wright 2003; Steffensmeier 1983; Steffensmeier and Terry 1986). As noted previously, Connell (1987, 1995) argues that masculinities are defined in relation to each other, but in relation to femininities as well. If he is correct, then how men view women will reflect back on their own images of self, and how they interact with women will be a key aspect of their gender construction efforts. Feminist ethnographies (e.g. Maher 1997, Miller 2001) indicate that violence is frequently used as a way to control women in this context. Thus, this book will examine men's interactions with women, with a particular emphasis on whether and how men use violence in their relationships with women on the streets. Further, close attention will be paid to how and when men discuss their own and others' use of violence against women.

However, men do not encounter women only in criminal street networks. They also interact with them in more domestically focused locales. Girlfriends and wives, as well as grandmothers, mothers, sisters and cousins, play some role in men's lives regardless of their level of embeddedness in streetlife. Following Wright and Decker's (1994, 1997) description of active offenders as 'urban nomads', it can be expected that these relationships will be tenuous and interaction infrequent. That does not mean that they are absent and without social influence on the men's behavior, including their violent behaviors. Broader work on mainstream masculinity has suggested that many men in the United States see a pivotal role demand as that of 'protector', especially with regard to female family members (Kimmel 1996). This may stimulate violence among the men in this study, or, as discussed below, family ties may limit men's participation in violence. The analysis pays close attention to how men discuss their interactions with women in a non-streetlife context and how, when and why they discuss using or avoiding violence as a product of these relationships.[6]

Within criminology, life-course and peer-influence models suggest that men who become integrated into normative family networks reduce their offending. Sampson and Laub's work (1993) suggests that such relationships deter offending, especially when those ties occur within a strong romantic relationship (see also Laub, Nagin and Sampson 1998). Warr (1996, 1998 2002) suggests that such desistance is not a product of the relationship with a normative woman *per se*, but due to the ending of relationships with delinquent peers (but see Giordano, Cernkovich and Holland 2003). As all the men in this study were active offenders and deeply embedded in criminal social networks, total desistance was not found in the data. However, it was thought that the data might include incidents in which these sorts of influences might be seen – instances where the interviewee could have been, but was not, violent in response to a challenge. Such events were sought out within the data and carefully examined. In addition to marriage, fatherhood is another potential influence. While motherhood has been shown to be a key transition for women in discussing their desistance experiences, few men raise fatherhood as a key element of such processes (see Giordano, Cernkovich and Holland 2003; Giordano, Cernkovich and Rudolf 2002). In fact, among men and boys, research shows an overlap of risk factors that predicts both offending and non-marital fatherhood (Nurse 2002). Little evidence in the literature suggests that the assumption of parenthood status acts as a catalyst for either offending or desistance, especially in neighborhoods experiencing the effects of concentrated poverty. As these communities are largely gender segregated, and children themselves can be produced out of social interactions where men and women have oppositional goals (Anderson 1990, 1999), I would not expect paternal responsibilities to be high on the list of priorities of men heavily involved in streetlife. While the necessity of supporting a family is an oft-romanticized motivation offered for male offending, it is one few men themselves have articulated in previous research (see Wright and Decker 1994, 1997). Indeed, the overall influence of fatherhood on men's violent offending is unclear.

Black street masculinity

Much work with women offenders has highlighted the power of intersectionality in the structuring of gendered action. Race and ethnicity profoundly shape gender norms and expectations (see Daly 1997; Maher 1997; Simpson and Elis 1995; West and Fenstermaker 1995). The literature on masculinity and street violence suggests that similar forces are at work. Denuding streetlife interactions of their racial and ethnic context ignores broader structural forces that alter the definitions of masculinity and intensify the meanings of violence for men.

Davidson (1974) provided one of the earliest, nuanced linkages of ethnicity, masculinity and violence in the ethnographic literature. Studying Chicano prisoners housed in San Quentin, he centralizes the concept of *machismo*, Latino hegemonic masculinity, not only as the main worldview aspect that structures violence, but more broadly, the majority of the inmate experience. For example, he links most of the instances of violence (as well as most non-violent behaviors) in his research to face-saving demands of *machismo*, be it the product of an insult directed at the individual convict or a group he is affiliated with. Davidson ties the nature of *machismo* and the degree to which it is attended by inmates directly to experiences of poverty and other disadvantages experienced by Chicano immigrants.

Substantial research suggests that African-American men who reside in extremely disadvantaged urban neighborhoods are more likely than their white counterparts to legitimate the use of violence in certain circumstances (see Anderson 1999; Bailey and Green 1999;

Oliver 1994; Simpson 1991; Staples 1982). Oliver (1994: 143) indicates that many of the men he interviewed framed their use of violence as a form of informal social control – not only in response to predation but also to maintain street-based norms, especially those related to rules of respect. Other work goes so far as to suggest that violence is central to the generation and maintenance of a distinctly black masculinity that arises out of the unique history of racial oppression and persistent denial of access to legitimate avenues of mainstream masculinity construction that characterizes poor African-American communities. In such contexts, street reputation, pose and associated violence become central to black men's identities (Anderson 1999; Majors and Billson 1993; Oliver 1994; Staples 1982).

Conclusion

Recent trends within the study of both gender and of crime have established that an understanding of the intersection of masculinity and violence requires a complex and specifically situated analytical framework. This volume explores how gender structures within streetlife social networks of the criminal underworld in the US frame the expectations and actualities of violence. It describes the contours of both hegemonic and subordinate masculinities on the streets and explores how these value structures undergird episodes of interpersonal violence. These normative codes must be understood within the context of de-industrialized, racially segregated US cities. The hegemonic form of street masculinity explored in these pages is a direct product of global, national and local forces coming together to shape life on the streets.

Notes

1 As I will show, once one understands the links between masculinities and violence, viewing these categories as mutually exclusive and distinct becomes problematic. For example, though the primary motivation for robbing a drug dealer may be the instrumental acquisition of drugs and cash, it also fulfills expressive functions of masculinity activation through exhibiting power in the process of dominating the victim. Similarly, although violent revenge may be motivated expressively by anger or shame, it serves the instrumental purpose of re-establishing street reputation that can instrumentally prevent future victimization.

2   Some would attribute the genesis of this line of work to Sellin's (1938) concept of culture conflict, which argued that law is a representation of the values and behaviors of a given society's dominant culture. Criminality was attributed to people holding different cultural values. Most of Sellin's examples, however, focused on problems of immigrant adaptation to a new society and culture rather than on the processes of subcultural formation within a class structure.

3   More recently, the work of Willis (1977) and MacLeod (1995) presents similar interpretations of violent and otherwise defiant behavior as a form of resistance to mainstream social values and expectations.

4   However, Anderson also claims that women in these neighborhoods increasingly adopt the code.

5   Of course, the street is not the only social location that Messerschmidt argues can produce crime as a form of masculinity construction. The family and the office are also suitable locales, but are out of the purview of this book.

6   The exception here is domestic violence, which will not be examined here because the data did not explore it. The interviews focused on street crimes and activities, not domestic relations.

Chapter 2

Gender's omnipresence: methodology

Ascertaining the nature and extent of masculinity's intertwinement with street violence is a complex endeavor that is not possible with strictly quantitative methods of social inquiry. It involves a rich understanding of the emic cultural maps that are carried around in the minds of criminally prone men deeply embedded in streetlife social structures and networks. Such cognitive frameworks are only accessible via qualitative inquiry. This study utilizes secondary analysis of previously collected interviews with active offenders to explore the nature of gender's interaction with and influence upon men's violence in a streetlife social context. The sample of interviewees used here was created through the combination of four previously existing interview studies done in Saint Louis, Missouri. The original studies were designed to elicit information about the accomplishment of specific offenses (e.g. drug robbery, carjacking, snitching and criminal retaliation); original analyses were phenomenological in nature and focused on issues such as motivation, target selection and enactment. For the current investigation, each interview was analyzed for gendered rhetoric and behaviors that were related to perspectives, and the accomplishment, of these street-focused behaviors. Understandings were built inductively from the interviews, then linked back to the existing theoretical and empirical literature.

This chapter begins with an overview of the research site, Saint Louis, Missouri. It then details the methods used in the project, explaining how the combined sample was constructed, key limitations within the secondary analysis as it applied to this project and how those limitations were overcome, and how the nature of the analysis was carried out.

The research site

The interviews used here were collected in Saint Louis, Missouri, a moderately sized Midwestern city. This city provides an excellent site for investigation as it is highly racially segregated (Massey and Denton 1993), hit hard by de-industrialization, and has experienced substantial levels of white flight since the 1960s (Suarez 1999). These forces generate neighborhoods burdened with conditions of concentrated poverty and disadvantage (Wilson 1987), known to produce strong streetlife social networks (Anderson 1990, 1999). Saint Louis is somewhat unique among US cities as its political boundaries have been firmly established since the nineteenth century. Unlike other urban areas, Saint Louis has not been able to expand its municipal territories through expansion and annexation. The metropolitan area, consisting of Saint Louis city, Saint Louis county and the collar counties (including abutting counties on the Illinois side of the Mississippi river) has an estimated population of 2,551,156. In the year 2000, the city itself had a population of 338,000; 46 per cent of households were white, 53 per cent were African-American, with a median age of 33.8 years. Over half the population had a high school diploma or less; 20 per cent of the city's population were living below the federal poverty line. The unemployment rate, 11.8 per cent, was more than three times higher than the national average. Nationally, the median age for all people in the US in 2000 was 35.3, with 80.4 per cent possessing a high school diploma. The aggregate unemployment rate of the US that year was 3.7 per cent with 12.4 per cent of all households in the US earning incomes below the federal poverty line (US Census Bureau 2000).

In 2001, the Saint Louis city police received 53,356 reports for index crimes. Violent crimes occurred at a rate of 2,332.5 per 100,000 population. Violent crimes reported are as follows: 148 murders (36.3 per 100,000), 105 forcible rapes (32.8 per 100,000), 3,140 robberies (943.5 per 100,000), and 4,256 aggravated assaults (1,309.9 per 100,000). The same year, the department made 112 arrests for homicide (103 male), 115 arrests for forcible rape (all male), 812 arrests for armed robbery (772 male), 3,183 arrests for aggravated assault (2,681 male). Nationally, the violent crime rate per 100,000 population was 506.1. The breakdown of rates per 100,000 population for specific index violent crimes was:

murder 5.5, forcible rape 32, robbery 144.9, aggravated assault 323.6 (Federal Bureau of Investigation 2002). Even compared with other cities, these are some of the highest rates in the nation by population size. Throughout the 1990s, and into the twenty-first century, Saint Louis has served as an active research site for ethnographic researchers gathering qualitative data on offending and offenders.

Disadvantage, neighborhoods, and crime

Most interviewees in the current samples were drawn from highly distressed urban neighborhoods displaying racial segregation, high unemployment, high levels of public assistance receipt, and high levels of poverty. As Wilson (1987, 1996) and Anderson (1990, 1999) have shown, such neighborhoods are often limited in the number of legitimate educational and work opportunities and are populated largely by single parent households. Such communities are home to streetlife social networks, often dominated by a culture of desperate partying (Shover and Henderson 1995; Shover and Honaker 1992; Wright and Decker 1994, 1997) but also characterized by competition between the streetlife-focused values and more mainstream aspirations and behaviors (e.g. see Anderson 1999). The last 25 years of the twentieth century were not kind to the city of Saint Louis proper. As discussed in Chapter 1, the United States core economy drastically shifted in the last part of the twentieth century; manufacturing jobs were widely replaced with service jobs. Saint Louis was not immune to this processes, in fact, the African-American members of the broader Saint Louis metropolitan region felt the pains of de-industrialization most strongly. To understand why de-industrialization had such a strong effect particularly upon the African-American population of Saint Louis, we need to understand a process which began earlier in the century: the gradual, but steady, exodus of whites from the core urban area.

As with most major cities in the United States, the city began to experience a loss of population in the post-World War II era as people moved to the newly emerging suburban areas. Buoyed by the combined forces of a healthy industrial economy, innovations in home construction technologies, the widespread availability of low-interest home loans provided by the GI Bill, and the ever expanding Interstate highway system created by the Eisenhower administration (which was initiated on the shores of the Missouri river immediately west of the city of Saint Louis in the building of I70), residents poured into outlying cities such as Florissant Valley, Saint Charles, Clayton and

Chesterfield. However, this population had one large demographic similarity – its whiteness. A number of social forces prevented African-Americans from making the same move.

This population exodus began during a period in US history where legal, structural racism was the norm throughout the county. The 1950s and early 1960s, which saw the first explosion of what sociologists and urban historians now call 'white flight', were a time when so-called 'Jim Crow' laws were in force throughout southern states. African-Americans went to separate schools, lived in separate neighborhoods, ate at separate restaurants and used separate public toilets. At this time, the major transformations of US racial social structure – the Civil Rights Acts and their upholdance by the Warren court – were still a few years away. Non-whites in the city who sought to take advantage of the economic boom years and move out of congested and increasingly dirty and crime-ridden cities were met with several legal and cultural barriers.

Before a series of US Supreme Court rulings in 1968 and 1969, it was perfectly legal to practice racial discrimination in the housing industry. For a black family seeking to move to the suburbs, this would manifest itself in a number of ways. The practice of steering was (and remains) rampant among real estate agents. Within the US, most home-buyers work through licensed realtors who work on a commission system. Prospective buyers find an agent, who garners a list of the buyer's desires in terms of size, location, etc. Then the agent shows potential buyers various properties that meet the criteria. This gives realtors a strong gate-keeping function within housing markets. Potential owners typically only see the properties that agents show them; agents show them houses in neighborhoods that look like the buyers. Blacks are shown homes in black neighborhoods; whites in white neighborhoods. While this is a direct violation of federal equal housing law today, it was legal during the first stage of white flight. Many African-Americans were simply not shown homes in the growing suburbs, but steered back into city neighborhoods.

Restrictive covenants were also a very popular tool of legal segregation in metro area housing markets. Simply, a restrictive covenant is a clause inserted into a home's sale contract that stipulates if the buyer of the property later sells the real estate to a member of a given group (here, African-Americans), the ownership of the property reverts back to the original seller. Such amendments were legal until 1968 and were widespread in the area.

Even those who did manage to navigate the legal maze of restrictive covenants and racist realtors were met with disdain by their new neighbors. Chilly receptions, slashed automobile tires, broken windows and a few instances of the infamous cross burnings were all used to drive out black residents from the growing suburban realms.

Thus, through the middle twentieth century, the city of Saint Louis itself became more and more racially homogeneous, especially the north-side. When the manufacturing economy of the United States began to decline, especially in the so-called 'rust belt' of major Midwestern and Ohio river valley cities, those individuals within the city were predominantly minority and disproportionably felt the pains that de-industrialization would bring. Many corporations began to relocate their operations out of urban neighborhoods that were becoming defined as increasingly undesirable – at the start of the process more out of the racial composition of the residents than any overt quality of life issues. Beginning in the 1970s and becoming increasingly intense through the 1980s and early 1990s, US manufacturing began to move assembly and processing operations to developing nations to take advantage of cheap labor pools and legal environments with less restrictive workplace and environmental regulations. Simultaneously, they began to move their white collar employees into office complexes in suburban regions, taking advantage of proffered tax abatements and appeasing the desires of their managerial employees to be closer to home and to avoid the economically suffering urban neighborhoods.

The loss of solid, working-class waged manufacturing jobs began a process of destabilization of urban neighborhoods. Obviously, the loss of factory jobs created a new class of unemployed persons; the effects quickly became more far-reaching. With the loss of factory workers' pay, the secondary economy of grocers, delis and taverns suffered, leading to more unemployment and loss of potential jobs. The severe reduction in income led to a reduction in the ability of the city to provide adequate public services like education, as well as a reduction of fire and police protection. Crimes rates inched upwards. Those economically capable of doing so moved to the newly vacated inner-ring suburbs, as whites were still fleeing ever outwards from the city, creating a second ring of suburban towns even further removed from the increasing disorder of the core city.

Walking through the neighborhoods of north Saint Louis at the time this data was collected presented a near stereotypical picture of US urban decay. Most residences were in various states of disrepair; collapsing abandoned buildings were to be found on every block – some of them had trees growing up through their centers.

The local economy consisted of quick stores, liquor stores, taverns, pawn shops and take-out restaurants, most of which had their windows and doorways barred for protection. Increasingly, clerks hid themselves behind sheets of bulletproof glass to deter robbers. They were neighborhoods that had not benefited from the economic improvements that the US experienced through the 1990s. There was little in terms of an influx of capital to help rebuild and restabilize life and economies. The men and women interviewed in the studies discussed in this volume have lived most, if not all, of their lives in these disintegrated urban environs. As I explore in the next chapter, it is in this milieu that both masculinity and violence took on new meanings and forms.

The sample

The sample in the present study was drawn from four separately collected interview projects done in Saint Louis over a five-year period: drug robbers were interviewed in 1998 and 1999; carjackers in 2000; snitches in 2001; and retaliators in 2002 and 2003. After removing cases for various reasons (see below), the total sample is 110 cases (86 men, 24 women). The interviewees were all African-American. The drug robbery sample contributed 26 cases (22 male, 4 female); the carjacking sample contributed 15 cases (11 male, 4 female); the snitching sample contributed 16 cases (12 male, 4 female); the retaliation sample contributed 42 cases (35 male, 10 female); eight cases were combined from multiple interviews of the same respondent in different samples (6 male, 2 female). The mean age for the sample was 28 years, with 15 being the youngest and 59 being the oldest. The median was 25 and multiple modes (24, 25, 26). The males and females did not differ appreciably in age. The mean for the males and females was 28; the median for males was 25 and 26 for females (see the Appendix for a full detailing of sample members by key characteristics).

While secondary analysis of existing data is quite common in quantitative studies, it is rarer within qualitative work (but see Sampson and Laub 1993). The actual merging of data sets for secondary analysis is even rarer, both quantitatively and qualitatively. A scarce few examples of this technique can be found in the healthcare literature (Heaton 1998). However, these studies involved the merging of only two data sets, with similar foci, and the researchers had been involved in the collection of data originally. To date, there has not been an attempt to combine so many data sets, collected with different research questions and goals.

A rationale for combining these potentially disparate samples is required. The data sets for this project were chosen from existing data collected by researchers at the University of Missouri–Saint Louis. They were all originally collected to study the accomplishment of specific offenses: armed robbery of drug dealers (see Jacobs 2000), carjacking (see Jacobs, Topalli and Wright 2003), snitching (see Rosenfeld, Jacobs and Wright 2003), and criminal retaliation. Two primary investigators, professors in the Department of Criminology and Criminal Justice, were involved in the collection of all of these data sets, though other researchers assisted in the data collection on two of the projects. A graduate assistant and post-doctoral fellow at the University of Missouri–Saint Louis participated in the carjacking interviews. A third professor in the department collected data in the snitching data set. This overlap of investigators produced a high degree of similarity within the data sets in terms of rapport, interview style, and the nature of probes and follow-up questions.

While obtained at different times, all the samples drew on the same social and geographic region: African-American neighborhoods in north Saint Louis that have experienced significant concentration of disadvantage. The same fieldworker was used in all the projects and some of the interviewees were sampled in multiple projects. While they represent different informants at different times, they are all essentially drawn from the same population (e.g. predominantly working- and lower-class criminally involved African-Americans in Saint Louis). Additionally, as detailed elsewhere in this chapter, the original plan was to include additional samples from Saint Louis; these were subsequently removed because preliminary analyses revealed that they represented slightly to significantly different populations. The samples that remain in the investigation hung together strongly: unless one is looking at the master sample list, one cannot easily identify which of the original samples a given interview was from. Since most of the offenders here were 'smorgasbord' offenders, meaning they engaged in a wide variety of crimes depending upon currently present opportunities, it is not always possible to identify a respondent's sample by the discussion of a specific crime type. Retaliation or snitching events are discussed in the context of interviews about robbing drug dealers or snitching and vice versa. Such topical crossover reinforces my choice here to present these interviews as a single sample.

A potential drawback is that the data were collected over the course of just over five years. Yet there is no indication within the data (or in other research) to suggest that the nature of streetlife in general, or the issues related to gender and streetlife specifically, have changed substantially within the time the interviews were collected. The neighborhoods experienced no major economic or social renaissance, nor any major reorganization of street crime patterns that were not already under way at the time of the first samples (for example, crack use and the crack trade were undergoing significant decline during the period, but this process was well under way by the time of the drug robbery interviews. See Jacobs (1999) for a full discussion of the street crack trade in Saint Louis and its decline in the 1990s.) Additionally, other major qualitative projects in the field have been carried out over similar time-frames (see Anderson 1999).

For all of these data sets a modified version of snowball sampling was used to build a sample (see Jacobs 2000; Wright *et al.* 1992). Initial contact with the interviewees was made through a fieldworker, who brought the respondent to the interview location. The fieldworker was present during all of the interviews. In some of the interviews, he interjects comments either on his own or when asked by the interviewee. In others, there is no record of him in the transcript. The original collectors indicated to me that he was present at all interviews, frequently at the bequest of the interviewee. After the interview was completed, the researchers asked the interviewee if they knew anyone else who was appropriate for the study. Some of the individuals were interviewed in more than one study. Only in the criminal retaliation study was a single person interviewed more than once in the project.

The interviews in all the data sets followed an open-ended interview protocol, that primarily focused on issues surrounding motivation and accomplishment of the crime that the project emphasized. The questions were designed to elicit thick descriptions of criminal incidents, with interviewer probing respondents to get a fuller depiction of exactly what happened, who else was present (and the role they played), how the offense in question was carried out, the precise proximate and distant motivations, and, if appropriate, what was done with the proceeds of the crime. Additional demographic questions were asked at the end of the interview (e.g. age, educational attainment, marital status, parental status, work status). The interviews lasted from one to two hours; they were tape-recorded with the permission of the interviewee, then transcribed verbatim.

In these data sets, gender was *not* an express variable of interest. While all of the data sets made a deliberate attempt to oversample women, some were more successful in doing so than others and most of the interviews did not specifically ask questions about gender issues. While the retaliation data set contained questions in 24 interviews specifically designed to elicit incidents of inter-gender violence, broader worldview issues were neither elicited nor probed. Nonetheless, even in those interviews without an explicit focus on gender, the gender composition of criminal social networks, notions of gendered self-image and gendered motivations came to the surface of the narratives during descriptions of incidents. The men frequently used highly gendered language and, without being prompted, clearly tied issues of offending to gender identity, statuses and role performances (for other instances where this sort of approach has proved productive with data collected in Saint Louis see Mullins and Wright 2003 and Topalli 2005).

As stated, the studies seeking offense-specific information (drug robbery, carjacking, snitching and retaliation) were derived from snowball sampling procedures that involved an ex-offender recruiting respondents from the community. The same fieldworker was used in multiple projects; due to this, some subjects were interviewed in more than one study. Where this was the case, the various interviews were merged into one case for the current study. Such repeat informants were identified with the help of the primary investigators who collected the data. In most of the data sets, the street names used remained the same; age at interview was also collected for all of these subjects that allowed for cross-checking interviewees in different data sets. Through recourse to the master sample list here, their own field notes and memories, the original collectors were able to identify eight repeat interviews. It remains possible that a few repeat subjects have gone unidentified here. Since I am not conducting statistical analysis and am doing discourse-oriented analysis, this should not represent a strong threat to the reliability and validity of the findings. If a participant is represented here as two cases (the same person with two different street names) it does not substantially affect the analytical points made.

At the start of the project, data sets in addition to those discussed above were included. Interviews with armed robbers, gang-involved boys and girls, and interviews focused on adolescent violence were all available for inclusion. At various stages of preliminary analysis these samples were excluded. The armed robbery data set was the first one removed from the combined sample because (1) it had previously been analyzed for gender differences (e.g. Miller 1998) and (2) it was not possible to identify all potential interviewee overlaps (different street names were given and it used a different fieldworker than the other data sets). The interviews from that project were neither coded nor entered into the project as Ethnograph files. Originally, a large sample (of over 240 interviews) was compiled to ensure that there was enough data of relevance to the dissertation's aims; as it used secondary data analysis, it was not clear how much of the information of interest would be present in the combined sample. Bluntly, early on I erred on the side of caution to ensure adequate materials for analyses. The preliminary analysis showed that rather than there being too little data present, there was too much relevant data. With the wealth of data present, the focus needed to be narrowed to ensure that adequate attention was given to the issues under examination. After coding, initial data analysis and drafts of preliminary findings, the decision was made to eliminate additional data sets.

Certain data sets did not integrate as well as was hoped in the design stages of the project. I first decided to remove the adolescent violence data set. This sample contained a much younger and less criminally embedded group of individuals. It was also collected with a different purpose than the four data sets combined here. While in the preliminary findings these interviews did generate some cross-validation of themes, they were significantly different enough to pose a number of potentially unsolvable problems to the analysis overall (for instance, separating age from embeddedness from sampling artifacts). The gang interviews were removed next. The original rationale for including this data set was to increase female representation. While this data set contained useful information on young women's experiences, those experiences were specific to adolescent gangs and had been analyzed previously from a similarly situated feminist theoretical perspective like the one used here (e.g. Miller 2001). There was no need to recover that ground. The male interviews, while potentially useful, were thinner in information covered and less useful in the analysis; removing them did little to the overall nature and scope of data in the project. Further, once the adolescent violence data set was removed, this sample became the 'odd sample out', as the four remaining samples had been collected by the same individuals with very similar aims and techniques. This data set had different collectors, with different sampling techniques. Moreover, if included, the overall number of women from the gang data set in the current sample would be disproportionate and misrepresentative in the analysis.

With the topical focus set directly upon masculinities, the question of whether or not to include women in the final sample was raised.

Since the focus was on masculinities, and not femininities, including women in the sample seemed at the worst potentially problematic or extraneous at the least. However, after careful consideration, the decision was made to include the women in this project. Their interviews provide (1) a set of confirmatory data (to see if the processes, attitudes, etc. that men discussed were discussed by the women as well); (2) a source of information about the nature of masculinities as perceived by women – who, it was expected, would occupy a subordinate position in street networks (see Maher 1997; Miller 2001, 2002; Miller and Mullins 2006a, 2006b; Mullins 2006; Mullins and Wright 2003; Mullins, Wright and Jacobs 2004; Steffensmeier 1983; Steffensmeier and Terry 1986) and have something of value to say about the nature of gender power hierarchies; and (3) they were indeed parts of the original data sets as I obtained them. The decision proved fruitful, as the women's interviews ultimately produced useful data for analysis and theory-building (see later, especially Chapter 5). Moreover, comparative analyses did not identify problems for the overall analysis with the females included.

Limitations and how they were addressed

This project's methodological approach is not without its potential drawbacks. There are issues related to qualitative analysis in general and to the form of secondary data analysis used here specifically. First, the more general issues are explored, then the unique issues within this project are addressed.

Validity of data

Overall, there are concerns about the internal validity of qualitative materials gleaned from active offenders. Offenders may hide or embellish facts presented to interviewers. Especially when monetary inducements for participation are present (used in all four data sets), individuals may be inclined to fabricate incidents or to enrich minor incidents so they seem more noteworthy. Alternatively, however, it is well known that on the streets no one does anything for free. To get the interviewees to participate, such payments were necessary. Undoubtedly embellishments occurred in the projects used to create the combined sample. Those researchers collecting the data were well aware of this potential problem and countered by probing vague or inconsistent answers to elicit more specifics, even on occasion raising inconsistencies to the interviewees. Other techniques of confirmation were used in the interview process. For example, when the respondents mentioned sustaining an injury, they often removed clothing to show the scars (such non-verbal actions are recorded in the transcripts by an interviewer describing what was being shown). Additionally, when present, the fieldworker would occasionally interject comments or additional details about the incident being described. Even if a few of the individuals fabricated or elaborated upon a few incidents in the data set, the data set's size, as well as the fact that analysis focused on trends and patterns, giving no undue weight to any single incident or interview, reduces the problems caused by such distortions.

One of the strongest qualitative checks on the validity of data is the emergence of consensus among interviewees concerning the subject matter of the interviews. As broad themes emerged during analysis, and numerous subjects reported the same things in the same ways, I became more assured that I had tapped into valid categories of knowledge (see Weller and Romney 1988). While precise statistical tests were not possible, the very emergence of the themes and patterns discussed later in this book enhance the confidence that the data present captured issues of interest. (For further discussion of internal validity in these specific data sets as it applies to the original analysis done see Jacobs 2000; Jacobs, Topalli and Wright 2003; Rosenfeld, Jacobs and Wright 2003.)

Further, this analysis is not directly interested in the micro-dynamics of offenses themselves (e.g. how one goes about selecting targets and carrying out offenses), but the foreground and background role that gender plays in the structuring of the lived experiences of those interviewed. Bluntly, it is not of interest to me whether or not the carjackers provided a precisely accurate description of offense enactment; rather, I am interested here in how gender may mold motivation, enactment and resolution. In fact, the analysis here did uncover some blatant misrepresentations of incidents as they occurred. For example, one of the interviewees discussed being shot and, while in the hospital, convincing his relatives not to exact payback on the shooter. The interviewee claimed it was his job to get revenge, not his cousins or nephews. However, when the man's brother was interviewed, he claimed that he had taken vengeance for that shooting soon after it occurred. Both men's descriptions of the shooting were quite similar, but their point of divergence occurred over the issue of the retaliation. While a problem with the validity of the data, for analysis of events here these sorts of inconsistencies yielded significant information about the role of masculinities in retaliation (see Chapters 4 and 6).

This study is most interested in the images and categorizations of gender in streetlife networks. If the interviewees chose the interview encounter as a chance to present an exaggerated image of masculinity (or femininity) in the self-presentation, these potentially polemical representations of gendered self only highlight the images and structures of interest. In fact, the interview site was seemingly used by many men to present themselves as *men* to the interviewers. It allowed them to reconstruct and present criminal offenses and victimizations in such a manner as to highlight their own masculinity while at the same time giving them the ability to deny masculinity capital to those they were interacting with. While it was impossible to ascertain the truth of the some of the statements made, that did not matter as much as the ability to analyze how the interviewee presented gender as a central principle in their perception and reconstruction of events.

The interviewers for the projects drawn upon in the combined sample were conducted by white, male, middle-class college professors. The social location of the researchers stands in stark contrast to that of the interviewees themselves who were working- and lower-class African-American males. Potentially, this created a social situation where the respondents felt the need to establish their masculine capital strongly. They could have used the interview location to 'front' – overstating and embellishing their actions to appear more masculine and possessing of more 'juice' than they actually had. Presented with a group of middle-class men enacting their own masculinity via the enactment of their profession (e.g. being college professors doing research), the subjects may have felt the need to respond by enhancing their own street and masculine capital. This could have taken the form of exaggerating their own actions as well as demeaning the actions of others. However, the fieldworker, a lower-class African-American male, was present during all the interviews. This provided a check on the validity of the incidents described (frequently interviewees asked the fieldworker to jog their memories on event details) as well as the worldview presented. Additionally, this form of masculinity embellishment, where it occurred, enhanced the value of the data for this project as those worldview elements are the express interest of this study.

Generalizability of data

Due to the sampling procedures, this combined sample is not representative of all individuals, or even criminal offenders, within these communities. However, they do provide a reasonable cross-section of individuals with regard to age, gender, offenses committed and depth of criminal involvement – some of the key issues explored in this study. The main drawback to these samples individually, and as a collection, is the issue of generalizability. Indeed, this is not a problem unique to this study, but an issue with all qualitative work. Since only a comparatively small number of individuals were sampled, and this sampling was distinctly non-random, it is not possible to determine the representativeness of trends and patterns uncovered. It is possible that some of the trends explored here are, in fact, artifacts of the sampling process. Thus, my findings and conclusions may not be applicable to other communities within the Saint Louis metropolitan area (especially different racial and/or socio-economic groups). Further, application to other geographic areas is open to question. They may be generalizable to other African-American offenders in urban communities of concentrated disadvantage. However, care should be taken as other cities and other racial/ethnic minorities may experience these structures differently.

There are several ways in which qualitative researchers handle this problem. One primary way is cross-validation with other studies. When different studies by different researchers in variant locations uncover the same findings, confidence in generalizability is increased. As discussed throughout this book, much of what was uncovered during analysis corresponds to existing work. Further, as noted above, during an early portion of data analysis, samples were incorporated that were later removed. These data, collected by different researchers, with different research interests and focusing on a much younger age group, uncovered many of the same themes and patterns discussed here. The examination of that data, though not included in this study, does confirm that these attitudes, perceptions and processes are not limited in the Saint Louis area to the networks sampled in the projects that were analyzed.

Issues of secondary data analysis

Secondary data analysis, while common within quantitative criminology, is much rarer in qualitative studies. Two articles have recently appeared in the field of criminology using secondary analysis techniques to explore a sub-sample of larger data sets, looking for themes and patterns unanalyzed in the original studies (Miller 1998; Mullins and Wright 2003). Despite its infrequency, this methodology is gaining some favor in the health sciences literatures (e.g. Corti, Foster and Thompson 1995; Heaton 1998; Hinds, Vogal and Clarke-Steffen 1998; Santacroce, Deatrick and Ledlie 2000; Thorne 1998).

Hinds, Vogal and Clarke-Steffen (1997) identified four approaches to the use of secondary analysis with qualitative data: (1) using a different unit of analysis to guide re-analysis; (2) using the sample to extract a sub-set of cases for more focused study of the original subject matter; (3) reanalysis concerned with exploring a concept present but unexplored in prior analysis; and (4) using the data set as a basis for the refinement of data collection. Both articles mentioned above illustrate these points. Miller (1998) drew sub-samples from a larger existing data set to conduct a more focused study of gender differences in the enactment of armed street robbery. The original analysis of the data (Wright and Decker 1997) neither thoroughly attended to these differences nor drew upon existing feminist models to explain the findings. Thus, her work illustrates the potential of secondary analysis to expand and enhance existing interpretations of qualitative data and apply new theoretical questions and interpretations to existing data sets.

Any form of secondary analysis, be it qualitative or quantitative, presents challenges, some advantageous, some disadvantageous. In general, one advantage of secondary analysis is the reduction of human and financial costs. Data is expensive and time-consuming to collect and prepare for analysis. Further, similar to quantitative data, well-collected qualitative data sets should contain a wealth of information that goes unexplored in initial analyses. Thus reanalyzing data sets adds additional value to rather expensive research endeavors.

For this project specifically, secondary analysis was appealing for a number of reasons. First, as mentioned, two recent papers (Miller 1998; Mullins and Wright 2003) had shown it to be a useful approach in studying how issues of gender molded criminal offending. As discussed in Chapter 1, a significant gap in the current literature on masculinities and crime in the United States is the lack of studies done with large (or even moderate) samples. Most work is either theoretical in focus, with data used for the purpose of illustration (e.g. Collier 1998; Messerschmidt 1993) or has been done with very small samples (e.g. Collison 1996; Messerschmidt 2000; Sim 1994). Few systematic analyses done on a large number of cases have been presented in the literature (for an exception, see Adler and Polk 1996). With the data available, precedent for the method's utility and the gap in the literature clear, I decided that a secondary analysis of a combined sample could more thoroughly examine the interconnection of masculinities and crime. While a project that collected new information would have held utility and value, using secondary analysis as a first step has identified key issues and contours within street masculinity that will help shape a project focused on the collection of primary data.

That said, there are several drawbacks to secondary analysis. One significant problem is the fact that the secondary analyzer may not have been involved with the collection of the data – thus information gleaned from field observations or other first-hand interactions with the interviewees is not available. The easiest way to surmount this problem is for the secondary analyst to have contact with the collectors of the original data. That is what was done here; it was possible to discuss questions and issues with the original researchers as they arose. Whenever necessary, I was able to talk with the principle investigators on the project, as well as co-investigators (save the fieldworker). Such contacts proved invaluable, and here actually led to the correction of at least one gender misclassification in the data as it was received. Yet the overall value of the 'field' experience was not conveyed. While the original collectors could provide me with their perceptions and experiences, those were not easily translatable into the analysis here. With such *in situ* observations, I could have a basis for the comparison of the offender's verbal accounts with actual enactments. This could have provided a richer understanding of the contradictions that emerged in the data (see Chapter 6) as well as a fuller understanding of the ways in which violent encounters evolved and how and why some encounters may have been resolved non-violently. However, since this volume is most interested in worldview issues, this is not a fatal limitation. Even if many encounters on the streets played out differently from those described within the interviews analyzed here, the broader definitional and interpretive dimensions of street masculinity explored here still strongly shape the way that social actors view violent interactions.

Due to the nature of secondary analysis, true grounded theory analysis is not possible. I was unable to go back to the original interviewees and field sites to recheck information or get additional insights. As questions were uncovered, I was only able to reread the existing interviews. While I did so extensively, I still could not examine data that was not present. This highlights another problem within secondary analysis, present in both qualitative and quantitative data sets. Questions that are central to the secondary analysis may not have been asked, or asked in a different fashion. Essentially, this is a problem of missing data. As Hinds, Vogal and Clarke-Steffen (1997) point out, the data may be missing either because the phenomenon in question was rarely encountered or because of a lack of attention to it by the primary collectors. It may not be possible to determine the cause of the lack of data. However, through reference to existing literature as well as consideration of the goals of the original project, tentative hypotheses about the absences may be made. In this study, many of the crime-specific sets were 'silent' on some key issues and factors. For example, while about half of the retaliation interviews asked questions specifically related to gender, these questions were not probed as extensively as I would have liked. Men freely spoke about using violence against other men and about general prohibitions against using violence with women. When probed, many men would then admit that they used some violence against women, but commonly insisted that it was not as severe as it would be if the target was a man. The issue of what was or was not severe was not elaborated upon. There were also numerous statements that men made about how to control women, for example, one just had to 'put your foot down' and that would be sufficient. What that meant was not probed. As discussed in Chapter 6, this leaves the suggestion that men define 'violence' differently when it is applied to men in a street context as opposed to when it is applied to women (in either a street or non-street context).

Another area of frustrating silence in these data are the general absence of discussions of men's interactions outside of a streetlife context, especially those that would occur within family environments. While every interviewee was asked about marital status and the number of children they had, additional information was only interjected into the interview by the interviewee. Some did (see Chapters 3 and 5), but many did not. Thus, it is not possible to be as confident about these themes because I only have some interviewee-introduced discussions, and cannot say whether the attitudes and relationship patterns extend to those men and women who were silent about their families. This, and other similar instances, are addressed where relevant in the chapters that follow to highlight the limitations of the data on those topics.

While there was a general overlap in the methods used in each of the studies, some studies focused on behaviors that were more inclined to produce discussion of gendered structures and perceptions. For example, the snitch and retaliation samples explored behaviors that are seen on the streets as essential to gender construction and presentation. 'Real' men do not snitch, but they do stand up for themselves and others in the face of violent victimization or challenge. Thus, those two interview sets produced more relevant information than others. The drug robbery and carjacking data sets were more narrowly focused on motivation and event enactment and dealt less with contextual matters or events surrounding those crimes. While they did produce some important findings and discussions, especially in the realm of how masculine capital is generated and how masculine presentations of self enhance and are enhanced by criminal activity, overall they contributed less to the findings discussed here. Still, for example, the drug robbery data set produced some unique definitions of subordinate masculinities related specifically to the drug trade, that were not present elsewhere.

Analysis

Data analysis here relied heavily upon inductive models of reasoning common to qualitative analysis. Traditional deductive reasoning begins with broader understandings and theory on a given subject matter, that are translated into specific casual predictions that are tested with relevant data. While qualitative data does allow for traditional theory-testing approaches that predominate quantitative inquiry, such rigid approaches often do not allow the discovery of the unexpected. One of the strong values of rich, descriptive interview data is the ability not only to explore major trends within the data, but also to find sub-trends and thoroughly explore deviant cases. Inductive analysis begins with specific observations and then attempts to build more generalized understandings from those observations. Themes, commonalities and divergences are noted within the data and broader theoretical understandings are then built from those (see Babbie 1998; Spradley 1979).

Purely inductive work is rare; field observations and data analysis are always guided to some degree by the existing theoretical and empirical literature. Simply, one cannot observe and collect data on everything in a potential field site. Similarly, one cannot look for any and all potential categories and themes within qualitative data. Yet within the specific framework of a given set of research questions and theoretical boundaries, inductive analysis allows for both the discovery of the unexpected and for the exploration of nuance and contingency within the data. It is the latter strength of such work that proved most valuable in this project. While existing work has focused on the broad contours of how masculinities shape offending, a close reading of the data here allowed me to illuminate the more subtle influences and alternative approaches to a given situation to be defined and illuminated. For example, when approaching the data, I followed Connell's (1995, 1987) framing of masculinity and expected to find multiple masculinities within the data arranged in relation to each other within power hierarchies. Being familiar with literature on masculinity and street crime, I was prepared to look for expressions of toughness, independence and self-control within these structural frameworks. Nonetheless, the exact contours of street masculinity and the various subordinate masculinities that emerged in the analysis presented in Chapter 3 were built inductively via the analysis of men's discourse about their actions, the actions of others and their descriptions of events within the interviews.

For the purposes of this project, in-depth interviews served as an excellent source of data to investigate the worldview of men deeply embedded in streetlife. As offenders produce narratives about their actions in specific social environments, they are trying to 'account for what they do and why they did it' (Maruna 2001). Such imposed order on these events provide insights into the worldview the respondent is operating upon and highlight their core self-perceived identity (McAdams 1993, 2001). Current work on the sociology of accounts – people's descriptions of their actions – emphasizes that such 'accounts may reflect culturally embedded normative explanations … in producing their accounts, actors are displaying knowledge of the ideal ways of acting and ideal reasons for doing what they have done' (Orbuch 1997: 460). Thus in recounting instances of criminal behavior for the interviewers the men, and women, in the sample not only produced narratives of the factually specific structures of offense commission (the focus of the original projects) but also situated those accounts within the broader context street norms – including those related to gender. Hence I was able to draw out of these narratives the gendered structures behind and meanings ascribed to these behaviors by the social actors. Such rich, descriptive data would not be obtainable in any other way.

The data itself was coded in a two-stage process. This was a product of the large sample size and of the broad nature of the initial codes. Due to the large number of interviews in the sample, Ethnograph (v5.0) was used in the first stage of coding and analysis. The use of this package was limited to electronic coding of interview passages and the pulling of tagged quotations. The interviews were initially coded blindly; I did not know the sample of origin, age or gender of the respondent. A series of tags were created following the major theoretical issues discussed in Chapter 1: Gender Norms, those descriptions, language usages or explicit statements about proper or improper behaviors that were related to gendered behaviors; Doing Gender, described incidents where the interviewees were enacting gender demands; Gender Networks, descriptions or discussions of the gender composition of street-based and non-street-based interaction networks and the nature of interaction within them; Gender Negotiations, behaviors that were focused on circumventing or otherwise navigating gender hierarchies on the streets; and Other, a catch-all category that was used to tag passages or events that appeared to have a gender-relevant aspect but that did not fit expressly within the above categories.

Tags were inserted into digital copies of the interview transcripts. The discourse used in discussing one's own actions, the actions of others, general statements about the nature of life on the streets and specific events were all identified in the first coding process. Similarly coded tags were pulled from the entire sample during analysis, printed out and sorted. This produced literally hundreds of interview segments. For example, the gender norms tag produced over 500 quotes in and of itself. While at this stage, having read carefully through every interview at least once (though typically more), I was building a general understanding of key themes and patterns, the amount of data in front of me was still too large. To narrow my analytical focus, each set of interview segments was then set aside as a sub-sample for more detailed analysis.

The second stage of data analysis was done one sub-grouping at a time. I reread each interview segment, this time with the reassignment of identity to the tag. I knew the age, gender and sample of origin of each quote. Where necessary for full understanding of the segment, I reviewed the context of the quote within the original interview. From there, subcategories within the larger categories were generated. For example, when sub-coding the Gender Norms tags, categories relating to street masculinity, 'punks', mainstream masculinity, women, family and children all emerged. Such inductive building of themes allowed for the uncovering of key differences, divergences and contradictions within the data. As this second stage of coding proceeded, some quotes were discarded as too vague or irrelevant to the category in question (e.g. the theme was not readily apparent from the quote and context or there were numerous interpretations of the data that the interview context could not resolve); others were reassigned to other major categories (e.g. on reanalysis a given incident may have been a clearer representation of gender norms than a gender negotiation).

The generation of sub-themes within the data at this stage not only highlighted the existing breadth of emic perceptions of the category in question (e.g. in gender norms, the various masculinities existing on the streets of Saint Louis were uncovered and defined) but uncovered strong interpretive contradictions within the data over key behaviors or attitudes (e.g. whether or not it was unmasculine to sneak up on a target of a violent victimization). Such multi-staged analysis facilitated working through a large and diverse sample, as well as the organization of the study itself.

Chapter 3

Real men and punks: masculinities on the streets

This chapter explores the central tenants and dimensions of masculinities as enacted on the streets of Saint Louis by men heavily embedded in criminal streetlife. Earlier work has identified components of masculinity in general and street masculinity specifically (e.g. Anderson 1990, 1999; Collison 1996; Messerschmidt 1993, 2000; Miller 1958); men in general, but especially men on the streets, are careful to construct presentations of self that highlight masculine qualities. The focus here is upon the social norms and social role demands of street masculinity – the hegemonic form that masculinity took in the data here.

The findings here indicated that men (and women) who are deeply embedded in streetlife networks defined and enacted masculinity in a fashion variant from mainstream US society. While many of the core elements of masculinity were the same (e.g. independence, toughness, financial success), some of these concerns were refracted and intensified by criminal involvement and the perceived omnipresent threat of violence. The intensively focused nature of these behavioral demands was compounded by the lack of structural opportunities present in the communities these men and women inhabited. White flight and de-industrialization severely weakened primary social institutions (e.g. work, family and education), giving primacy to street norms.

Although these are broad patterns and themes uncovered within the data, my explorations uncovered sub-trends contradictory to the predominantly vocalized notions of masculinity. These will be fully explored later in the volume; this chapter examines general trends and emic understandings of street masculinity. We should realize that fulfilling these demands is neither easy nor straightforward. Contradictory role demands were prolific; role strains were incredibly common in the data. Additionally, lives characterized by deep embeddedness within criminality also presented many practical demands on behavior to avoid imprisonment, serious injury or death – these realities of life on the streets also frequently contradicted gender ideologies. When 'doing gender', the men in this sample attended to these multifaceted expectations, with situational factors dictating which sets of behavioral expectations took precedence.

Key elements of street masculinity

As discussed, much prior work has explored the interconnecting nature of masculinity and criminal activity. The data confirmed many existing findings about the nature of masculinity. The men in this sample were highly concerned with projecting images of toughness, independence, self-sufficiency and potential violence. Such street masculinity was framed by the social realities of sub-living wage employment, the perceived ubiquitous nature of violence and deep criminal involvement. In general, status hierarchies in mainstream US masculinities involve the utilization and display of key capitals (social, cultural, financial and gender) to establish your relation to others; the streets of Saint Louis are no different. However, the most common paths to capital acquisition (e.g. education and work) were either not available or were scorned by many of the men and women interviewed. Unlike much of the existing work on masculinities and criminal violence that focuses on adolescents and young men, the sample here is composed of *adult* men, both young and old. While Anderson (1990, 1999) looks at an entire community, most of his examples of violence concern younger individuals; similarly Messerschmidt's (2000, 2004) recent work is exclusively focused on teenagers' use of violence. For this reason, although not all of the themes discussed here are entirely new, the data is different in the much older population being interviewed.

Street names

During data collection, the interviewees were asked to provide a nickname or a street name that would be used to identify them in analysis of the data while protecting their identities. While some of the street names were mundane (e.g. Curly, Lewis, Slim), about half of the men gave clearly masculinized street names that highlighted attributes valued in street-corner life. Such names provide insight into self-perception and the form of identity they chose to present in the interview and on the streets. Some names emphasized a 'crazy', violent, or otherwise tough persona (e.g. Crazy Jack, CrazyJay, Looney Ass Nigger, Mad Dog, K-Ill, Block, Icy Mike and Loco). Others emphasized the excesses valued in a culture of desperate partying (e.g. Lil' Player, J-Rock, Binge, Playboy, Jhustle, Kilo, Player and Play Too Much). Others offered up a picture of untrustworthiness and underhandedness, at least from the perspective of mainstream values: Do Dirty, Lowdown, Sleezee-E, C-Low, Snake, and DL (Down Low).[1] The names chosen for self-representation highlight the extent that elements of street masculinity were integrated into the identity of those deeply embedded in criminal streetlife.

Independence

Being in control of your own actions, acting independently of others, and being self-sufficient were essential pillars of street masculinity. Men activating street masculinities emphasized the value of these qualities. Indeed these are part of broader American masculinities, but here they were manifested in an intensified form as a core set of gendered expectations. Unique conditions faced on the streets (e.g. frequent violent challenges, lack of other available gender capital, and the potential to be snitched on to the police) produced an acute focus on these traits.

Establishing the importance of self-control, Speezy explained, 'I feel like I'm in control of my own actions. You know, when I ain't with nobody, then, nobody can tell on me or nothing, so I can do what I gotta do.' Tall similarly said, 'I'm accountable for my actions, I know exactly what I'm doing it when I'm doing it … I look at it as a strength.' Spanky, responding to a question about where he lived, framed his homelessness as a form of masculine independence: 'I don't want to stay in one place too long … I don't want to get tired of being in somebody house, nagging and bitching and me there.'

As with many elements of street masculinity, serious practical considerations lay behind the emphasis on independence. Primarily, interviewees emphasized that other people would double-cross them, snitch on them, or do anything if they could profit from another's downfall. Independence from others on the streets became a response to the general lack of trust held among men on the street corner. This was fused with the strength of being able to stand on their own. When asked about having friends on the streets, Black explained, 'My mama is my only motherfucking friend. Dude, that is it, you hear me, ain't no friends. Ain't no nothing. You got people that's acquaintances – people will play you out ... your motherfucking family will play you out. OK. I don't put nothing past nobody, man, because all I know I can only control myself.' Bacca also emphasized that his social isolation was a product of the violence on the streets: 'The friends I do have been there for me are lost, they're dead. I feel like I don't have anything to lose.'

Wright and Decker (1994) describe how many burglars would take orders for specific goods from peers and family members, thereby reducing the uncertainty of getting rid of stolen goods after a breaking-and-entering. While a few of the men in the carjacking sample admitted to doing this as well, some of the men outright rejected this behavior, claiming that it infringed on their ability to be independent from others. When asked if he ever took orders for specific car parts, C-Ball replied, 'I don't do that. I don't do what nobody gonna tell me to do. I do it on my own. Be your own man.' For C-Ball, independence was framed as more essential than a certain market for stolen goods. Black proffered a similar reason, 'I don't want nobody knowing my motherfucking business. See, I'm gonna do what I'm gonna do. I'm just gonna be chilling by myself.'

Not only did men refuse an easy market for stolen goods, others even rejected the assistance of peers and family members in carrying out violent retaliations against those who had wronged them. The importance of independence and being in control of their own actions was clearly shown in the following exchange between an interviewer and Goldie. While discussing the results of being shot during a street altercation, he explained why he did not accept help from his family with the retaliation:

Goldie: When I got shot my nephew was out there going crazy, calling up saying 'What do you want me to do?' 'I want you to do nothing, just calm down, just go on about your life. [The] Doctor told me I'd be walking again, gonna still be happy, I'm gonna get them.'

Interviewer: But why is that, why did you have to do it yourself?

Goldie: 'Cause it was done to me, you know, like it might be somebody do something to my nephew. Most likely he not gonna want me to jump in, he gonna want to do everything on his own. So, if he do the crime he do

> the time, you know. Ain't no use everybody doing the time.

As Goldie showed, an important masculinity issue was at stake – the desire to respond to the injury personally as evidence of his self-reliance. Social network considerations also worked their way into the explanation – not wanting his nephew to go to jail for something that Goldie saw as his responsibility.

Such findings provided a contrast to existing work on issues of independence and its connection to masculinity found in work on adolescent street gangs. Youth heavily involved in streetlife activities emphasized the need to stay bonded as a gang for self-protection. Gang members speak frequently about 'having each other's backs' (for example, see Decker and Van Winkle 1996; Jankowski 1991). With age, independence from such bonds apparently grew more intense and significant. Men began to see it as more essential to stand on their own, potentially compromising their own safety or well-being to do so. This may be a function of age-grade cohorts ageing out of crime and the adolescent networks subsequently fragmenting, or simply a shift in attitude accompanied by years spent on the streets.

When asked if he had ever called upon or hired someone else to carry out a violent retaliation, Black indicated that not only had he never done such a thing, but would never do it, telling the interviewer, 'I take care of myself ... why spend the money for it? ... I got a few little homies[2] out there who would do something. You know, I got some that would do something for free for me but then I'd have to owe them, and I don't want to do that.' Here, calling on others for assistance required the spending of either financial or social capital. Specifically, it created debts and obligations that reduced the independence Black would be able to exercise. Such social ties ran counter to expectations of independence and self-sufficiency.

Several men made direct connections between the need to be in control of their own actions and the desire to be independent of others by avoiding imprisonment. Cal said:

> That's [getting jailed] fucking horrible man, that's bullshit. For real, man, who'd wanna be locked up, man? Only a fool'd wanna be locked up, man. I'm not gonna lie to you, only a damn fool would wanna be locked up ... telling you when to wake up, when to go to sleep, how long you can stay outside. You a grown ass man, you don't want nobody telling you that

bullshit ... six months in jail, even three months ... in that same fuck ass place.

Beano expressed similar attitudes, but added a political tinge to his description: 'Freedom. That's the ... I mean we [African-Americans] fought so hard to break it, to get freedom, then somebody take it from you again, 'cause of you actions.'

Another component of independence and self-control is exhibiting power over others. When discussing their engagements in crime, many of the men in the sample highlighted how carrying out a criminal action, be it a violent assault or a violent acquisitive crime like robbery or carjacking, provided a social location for the display of control and self-empowerment. Many reported getting a 'high' or 'kick' from such actions (see also Katz 1988; Wright and Decker 1994, 1997). When describing how he went about accomplishing a carjacking, Snap emphasized, 'I'm in control, you know what I'm saying, get in the car, OK, alright, do what I say. Basically you will do what I say.' Kilo described how power was a central form of the presentation of self during the criminal event: 'You just look 'em straight in the eye and let 'em know you mean business and give it to me right now or tell me where else the stash is ... I want it right now. Tell me right now.' Both of these quotes exhibited the violent presentation of self essential to successfully conducting a street robbery. As other qualitative research has shown, this process is central to defining the nature of the social interaction between offender and victim (see Anderson 1999; Katz 1988; Wright and Decker 1997). Here it is important to note that these can be seen as extensions and activations of the masculine demands of self-sufficiency and independence – the ultimate form of independence is the ability to enforce one's will on someone else. This is clear when the offenders were describing the joy they received in this imposition of power on others.

Do Dirty said, 'It's fun. I love to see people run. I love to see them shake in they pants. I seen a dude shit and piss on hisself.' Junebug, when asked what his favorite part of a robbery was, replied, 'Just taking they money, seeing them scream, crying, begging, don't kill me ... it's fun to me. I like to see the motherfuckers scream.' Goldie's response to the question exhibited a similar attitude: 'Just seeing the motherfuckers doing what you tell them to do you know, get down, and they get down and shake a little. They be scared that I'm gonna kill 'em or something. They be scared of nothing, we just want to get they money so they don't get shot or nothing.' Smokedog described the kick he received when seeing his victims on the streets after the robberies: 'I be right in they face laughing and they don't even know I'm the one who robbed them last night … That's cold ain't it?' Such 'cold' bravado was a key aspect of street masculinity. Later in the interview, when discussing seeing someone on the streets he had shot, Smokedog said, 'No, he ain't dead. He didn't die. I shot him in the ass. He wearing a shit bag[3] though. Right now today he still wearing one, a shit bag. Every time he see me I start laughing and ride right on past him.' These responses emphasized the feeling of power street offenders gain from violent activities; in some ways, this was the ultimate expression of independence and self-control. A key aspect of masculinity was establishing yourself dominant over others. The above-quoted offenders not only used violent crime to fulfill this gendered demand, but obtained visceral pleasure from doing so.

Trust nobody

One key reason interviewees gave for maintaining their independence on the streets was the threat posed by street associates. Snitching, double-crossing, and setting people up for victimization were frequent realities these men faced. Direct or vicarious experiences with these factors quickly taught many men a cardinal rule of streetlife: trust nobody. C-Ball, when asked if he trusted his friends or co-offenders, emphatically said, 'No, you don't trust nobody in the ghetto anyway. Don't never trust no nigger that live in the ghetto.'

In discussing being double-crossed by a street associate and set up for a victimization, Don Love explained the lesson he learned about trust on the streets: 'You know, never put your trust in no motherfucker … I kind of trusted this cat 'cause I was young. You see, now it's a different program I'm running with.' Again, age surfaced as important. Don Love presented age as changing his attitudes in two ways. First, he accumulated necessary experiences as he spent more time on the streets; at the time of the interview, he was less naïve than before. Second, he implied that the very fact that he aged had altered the nature and organization of his activities. He was then operating with a 'different program'. The following exchange also strongly emphasized the problematic nature of trust on the streets and why street masculinity emphasized independence from others:

Block: It be the nigger you know who gets you. It don't be the nigger you don't know. It don't be the enemy dude that kill you – it be somebody else that kill you.
Interviewer: People that know of you but not really know you.

Block: Could be he know me –
Interviewer: But you're not friends with him, or you are?
Block: We cool, you know what I'm saying? It ain't even for
               real … It ain't like me and (the fieldworker) right there
               … motherfucker we sell work [drug dealing] to. We get
               high with. We go to a party. He at the party because
               we know the same people and that how we know each
               other.

Block identified his associates and acquaintances as the key source of danger on the streets. Big Mix offered another example of this: 'My friend is doing, like, two years in [federal prison] for him snitching on her and it's like they were so close you never can trust … you never really can trust nobody. They was close, they had known each other for like eight years.' Bacca discussed a relationship with a co-offender in the following way: 'We're friends but we're already at the point where we don't trust anybody … right now I'm on my own, I don't have any friends, I don't trust nobody.'

When asked about his relationship with his co-offenders, Smokedog said, 'I don't trust them. I really don't trust nobody for real, to tell you the truth. But if my little partners know where some dope at and they want to do it with me or they … put me up on they scam, they didn't have to put me up on it, they could have did it theyself.' The critical practical issue that dictated not only male independence of others but also avoided trusting others on the streets was the potential to be snitched on by people who know what you have done. Geasy indicated trust only existed between family members: 'Fuck the dude [any potential co-offender], he [will] always fuck you over first … Ain't your blood, real people. If you never grew up with them you can trust them to a certain extent but you can't [really trust them].'

Similarly, Sleezee-E described how he coped with the prevalence of snitching:

Sleezee-E: Yeah. I'm worried about being snitched on.
Interviewer: So how do you change that?
Sleezee-E: How do you change that? You don't ever have anybody
               with you that you can't trust and you never do nothing
               with somebody. You always do it alone.

Likewise, TD bluntly stated, 'If I get held by the police and all that by myself I won't tell on myself … I can't tell on myself.' And Do Dirty explained that he worked alone, 'Because I'll never tell on myself ... my friends don't even know that I do robberies.' Overall, these realities created a strongly verbalized belief about never snitching to the police on anybody, despite the fact that snitching was a very common practice (see Rosenfeld, Jacobs and Wright 2003).

While the older, more experienced members of the sample emphasized that 'you can't trust anyone', younger members of the sample berated snitches and claimed strong levels of trustworthiness. As discussed above, the older men were less tied to street associates, while the younger interviewees were more tightly bonded to their criminal peers:

Little Rag: You can't ever snitch on your partners. If you snitch on them you can't ever be trusted no more.
Interviewer: What about an enemy, you know, a rival?
Little Rag: No, I would never do that ... No, no. Anyway, I ain't got no enemies. I'm, how you say, one of those people. They know you so everyone say you're cool. I just kinda like people.

Cal expressed similar sentiments: 'Shit, I'm not snitching on some of my friends when I'm out there doing the same thing. You crazy? So [the police] asked me, but man that's some bullshit, I ain't telling on nobody and I'm saying I ain't taking the witness stand. I don't give a fuck man, I ain't snitching on nobody, man.' Dog also emphasized that he would never snitch: 'No, never, no, I'm not the telling type. I don't tell on nobody. That's in my blood, you know, it's just like if you and me are together and we get a robbery with someone and you get away with it and they catch me, why am I gonna tell on you because you got away?' Presenting yourself as trustworthy, especially among younger interviewees, emphasized the valued masculine qualities of strength and reliability. This was most likely due to the stronger tendency for younger men to operate in groups; they saw those groups as essential to their criminal success.

Despite the emic denials of involvement with the police, snitching was commonly discussed in the interviews. Smokedog described when he found it acceptable to snitch:

They're [the police] like, 'We want that gun. If we can't get that gun then we gonna have to give your girl three years' and shit like that right. So I'm like, man. And the dude, the dude, man, who I was fucking with man, he ain't one of the homies, you know what I'm saying. We didn't grow up together, we didn't throw rocks together, we didn't climb trees together, we didn't play catch a girl, get a girl together. We didn't do none of that shit. So fuck him … (mentions man's name) got that gun. Yeah. (The man's name) got the gun.

Smokedog highlighted some key lessons learned from spending time on the streets: snitching would happen and you had to protect yourself and your very close network associates. No one else deserved protection, in part because they were likely to give you up as well.

Fatalism

A profound sense of fatalism permeated the interviews in this sample. Asked whether he worried about being fatally victimized for his street endeavors, Jhustle said, 'When it's my time to go, it my time to go. It going down one day. It's just going down one day.' In such a violent, uncertain world this was not very surprising; in fact, Miller (1958) identified fatalism as a focal concern among the offenders he worked with (see also Shover 1996). These views reinforced violent actions and reactions to others, supporting the broader tendencies toward violence on the streets. Such attitudes appeared most frequently when the respondents were asked about their fears concerning counter-retaliation, but they were present to a lesser degree throughout the interviews.

A sense of the inevitability of being victimized was overpowering, leading many of the men to metaphorically, and literally, shrug their shoulders and say they simply were not concerned about it. Player succinctly said, 'Well, you really ain't gonna have no fucking choice if it happens. Its outta your hands.' Play Too Much explained, 'No, I'm not worried about that … I just let that be … I mean, no, I don't care. It comes down to that, it comes down to that.' Lafonz said, 'You get used to it after a while. You can't go around being worried about shit like that. It'd just fuck your head up … worrying about having to, you know, watch over your shoulder all the time.' The men here knew they were going to be violently victimized, even killed, because of their involvement in criminal activities, accepting this inevitability as a key part of their cognitive map of the streets.

In discussing the ever-present threats and actualities of violence, many of the men referred not just to a cycle of violence, but to their own broader embeddedness in crime. Goldie, who had been severely injured in several violent encounters over the years, explained why he was not concerned about people coming back at him. When asked if he was worried about an impending counter-retaliation, Goldie said, 'Not at all ... because you know, I just do so much dirt to a point that one day my time is gonna come ... [it is] just not in my mind [to] worry at all. I just got to be myself and just do what I got to do.' Responding to a similar question, Big C made similarly broad, fatalistic claims: 'Life is too short these days. You know, you never know. I could walk out this door here and fall over. Might not even wake up. I could go to sleep tonight and may not even wake up, so I don't even trip on it.' Bacca drew an analogy with what he saw as a frequent childhood experience: 'It's just like a kid going in his mother's dresser and taking her money without asking and he know he's gonna have to suffer the consequences later. I just have to suffer the consequences. I'm not worried about anything. I don't [have] anything to lose. I feel like I have a lot to gain but I don't have nothing to lose.' C-Ball bluntly said, 'You gonna die anyway.' Later in the interview he elaborated, 'I live in the ghetto and I'm gonna go out and do bad 'cause I was raised up around that. So I ain't scared of death, I know we all gonna die one day. I don't care about this world.' K-Red made a similar connection to the inevitability to death: 'I don't need to worry about it. I know we all gonna die soon, why worry about it ... we all gonna die pretty soon, we all gonna die. We don't stay on Earth forever. We all gonna die.' Big Mix concurred: 'Cause I just don't give a damn. I don't care what happens, really. I don't care, what else. That's how it always is, or whatever. Whether they kill us or whether we kill them, some don't shake [in fear of being victimized].'

Some of the elements of fatalism proffered by the interviewees were also distinctly tied to religious notions. Red explained why he was not concerned about people retaliating on him for his actions: 'I ain't worried about it, man, 'cause, I mean, God put me on this earth to live my life. I'm not dead. If the Bible got me, it got me. I'm not afraid of it, but if you hit me and miss me then [you] better be scared.' Do Dirty made a similar connection: 'I go home at night and go to sleep and might not even wake up no more for the rest of my life. If God call me, he call me. But I can say one thing about it, I had a damn good life and I enjoy everything that I do.' Such attitudes formed a core part of the cognitive map men on the streets used to guide their lives and actions. Certainly, embracing fate and inevitability reinforced norms of toughness and independence. A man who worried too much about the consequences of his actions and the inevitability of counter-retaliation appeared weak and potentially scared of other people. Conversely, allowing fate or God to determine the outcome of his life established a rough, stoic worldview that easily fit in with other elements of street masculinity. This should not be taken wholly at face value. Most of the men, in other contexts within the interviews, did talk about watching their backs, sneaking around the neighborhoods when they felt like they were being directly pursued, carrying weapons and being sure to be in the company of peers they could trust in case they encountered someone they had wronged.

Work

For most working- and middle-class men in the United States, work is the primary tool used for the construction of adult masculinities. Jobs provide wages to support families, fulfilling the classic breadwinner conceptualization of masculinity (Connell 1995; Kimmel 1996) and to engage in conspicuous consumption; they also provide a key source of prestige, and are central to the way in which core American values of hard work and self-sufficiency are achieved. The vast majority of males in the sample here were not working at the time of the interview. Work interfered in many ways with deep participation in streetlife, especially the culture of desperate partying that characterizes life on the streets of Saint Louis (see Shover and Honaker 1992; Wright and Decker 1994, 1997).

All the interviews included questions about current employment and employment aspirations. The interview provided a social location where the offenders had to negotiate a potential masculinity challenge as they were confronted with their marginal workforce status by white, middle-class men who clearly actualized their own middle-class masculinity via their status as college professors. Many of the unemployed men here responded in such a fashion as either to reject the validity of work or to explain why the jobs they could get were not worth their time (see also Bourgois 1995, 1996).

The following exchange between Mo and the interviewer highlighted how other aspects of street masculinity interfered with typically working-class employment:

Mo: I don't want a job.
Interviewer: They'd want you to work for them.
Mo: I don't work for no one man. I lose interest fast.
Interviewer: Why is that?
Mo: I don't like listening to people, don't like people telling me anything.

Mo positioned independence as more essential than work to his masculinity. Others emphasized the low pay most working-class jobs in the Saint Louis area offered as the key reason they weren't engaged in full-time employment, especially when the street presented opportunities for what they saw as easy money. Slim explained:

> I don't have enough education to get the right kind of job that I want, you know, because why would I go into a job at $5.15 an hour, $5.25 an hour? Bust my ass from 7:00 in the morning all the way to around 2:00 or 3:00. Why would I do that there when I go out here and it take me about a day and I can knock off about $600, $700, $800 right there and in a week's time or a week and a half, that's gone, I'm back at it again.

Kow said, '[A legitimate job has] gotta be like paying you something. This $5.00 and $6.00 shit, no.'

Player was seemingly caught off-guard when asked if he worked. His rambling response to the simple question highlighted the tensions between work and mainstream masculinity and the realities of street masculinity:

> No, man, that's [a good job] what I need man, 'cause honestly, man, I ain't even trying to do this shit no more. It ain't no life … I don't want none of this shit, I don't. I do want a job … I really do want a job, man. Motherfuckers, they just getting hotter. 'Cause when you really want a job, 'cause I don't really want to work for real, 'cause I can make some money – but working is something I know is good for you and you really need to fucking work, but man, you really tripping me off, man, and I get scared. Oh fuck it and usually people that want a job get a job.

Notice how Player wavered between legitimizing legal work as a critical source of masculinity, especially when compared with the dangers of criminal involvement, but then retreated from the stance. Don Love, who throughout his interview proclaimed himself to be a central and powerful figure in the Saint Louis underworld, surprisingly discussed his attempts to gain entry to the world of legitimate work: 'I'm trying to get a temp service job 'cause I already know that's what I'm trying to do, keep my head above water. You know, keep people off my back because, you know, people be nagging.' Don Love seemed to be experiencing demands to fulfill mainstream masculinity from his intimate social networks.

Some of the offenders in the sample did work legitimate jobs, but also participated heavily in the underground economy. When asked why he engaged in armed robberies despite the fact that he worked a full-time job, Smokedog explained, '[I need to] get some more money. Ain't no punkass $5.50 an hour man, that ain't shit. I can make $300 in 10 minutes, 20 minutes or so.' Similarly, Play Too Much, who drifted between legal and illegal work said, 'What I do is fork-lifting and shit … I mean off and on. I ain't gonna say I keep a steady job for a long period of time … I gotta [keep a steady job]. I'm making ends meet.' Low explained the motivation behind his legitimate work: 'Now, it's not like I won't work, it's that I have to support my family with the checks I get through the temp service', while the proceeds from his criminal activity went to partying, drug use, and other hedonistic pleasures.

The isolation of many of the men in the sample from mainstream culture and aspirations, whether they involve issues of masculinity or not, was clear from how little the men discussed engagement in these activities and social locations. As seen above, some of the men alluded to mainstream aspirations but did not see such structures as open to them. While they were keenly aware of the demands of mainstream masculinity, with some discussing feeling social pressure to display those traits (e.g. Don Love's complaint of people 'nagging' him; Player's insistence that 'you really need to fucking work'), resources necessary to 'do gender' in that way are not available (e.g. education and work).

Punks

Connell (1987, 1995) points out that any hegemonic set of gender demands is defined in opposition to various subordinate statuses. In the case of hegemonic street masculinity several subordinate masculinities existed. The most clearly recognized and most frequently discussed subordinate masculinity among men on the streets was that of the 'punk' – someone who demonstrably failed to live up to the demands of street masculinity. The term punk entered the language of the streets from prison environments. In prison, a punk is someone who receives anal and oral sex, often doing so by force or to gain the protection of another inmate (Kupers 2001). They represent a key subordinate masculinity in prison culture. As in prison, on the streets punks were men unable to stand up for and protect themselves. It was not surprising to see a crossing of terms from the prison to the street because of the large number of men on the streets who have done time.

Linguistically and cognitively, the category of punk is linked to both femininity and male homosexuality. Men associated with the descriptive punk were seen as being soft, womanly, a 'bitch', or a 'fag'. Hops expressed this clearly by saying, '[If] you let one motherfucker get over on you and [people on the street] find out, you know what I'm saying, another motherfucker will get over on you. So it's gonna be like [people on the street will] label you as a punk.' Smokedog presented a similar description: 'I ain't got time to be playing there, man … This shit out here dog, if you let one motherfucker punk you, man, every motherfucker gonna try to punk you … no nigger's fucking with me.' Similarly, Moon explained why he spent so much of his time looking for the men who had shot his uncle:

Interviewer: What if you didn't go over there and do what you did?

Moon: Then they'd think you punks.

Interviewer: Wouldn't they think you're a punk, though, 'cause you didn't get the guy who shot your uncle?

Moon: No, man, no. No, we went over there. Just to let them know that we ain't gonna let them fuck with us like this.

Here, even though a violent retaliation wasn't carried out successfully, Moon presented his and his family's behavior in such a way that street credibility was re-established through the willingness to go into a hostile neighborhood, even if they didn't find the actual perpetrator.

Simply, punks were not a threat to a man's safety and masculinity. As Paris clearly stated when asked if he was afraid that someone he had victimized would retaliate against him, 'He's a punk. Ain't nothing to be scared of. They're scared of me.' In talking about the target of a carjacking, C-Ball described him as, 'scary, he was a scary little punk. Do you know what a punk is? He don't know how to fight, he don't know how to do nothing, he scary.' Bacca also explicitly made this connection:

Interviewer: Was this a dangerous guy?

Bacca: No … He's a punk.

Interviewer: Just not hard?

Bacca: That's what I'm saying, just not hard, just a punk … a wannabe.

All these excerpts frame punks as failed men, as men unable to actualize the rigorous demands of street masculinity especially as it is framed within potential and actual violence. Yet, just as there is more to street masculinity than successful fighting, there was more to punkness than being soft or weak.

There was some substantial disagreement among interviewees as to what constituted punk behavior. Several men indicated, for example, that they thought that the use of guns was a 'punk move': if you were really a man, you would use your fists, not a firearm. This stood in stark contrast to the ubiquity of guns on the streets and the large numbers of men who described using firearms in their criminal activities. One interview exchange highlighted this tension, making it clear that this was a contested hegemonic belief on the streets. In the following section several interviewers were present, with the interviewee (Sleezee-E) and the fieldworker (Smokedog):

Interviewer: So you guys did not have a gun?
Sleezee-E: No, we [n]ever carry a weapon. That's only for wimps.
Interviewer: So you only need a gun to take some shit from somebody?
Smokedog: [interrupting] So I guess I'm a motherfucking wimp.
Interviewer: [to Smokedog] Because you are always strapped, right?
Smokedog: Great. I guess I'm a wimp then.
Sleezee-E: I can't use no gun, man. A gun is more federal time, more jail time if you get caught.

Smokedog challenged Sleezee-E's notion of hegemonic masculinity. This was the only place in this interview[4] where Smokedog spoke up; clearly he took umbrage with being labeled a punk, especially in front of the interviewers. As a form of face-saving behavior, Sleezee-E quickly qualified his expressed attitude as a function of self-protection and imprisonment avoidance.

Punks as targets

In discussing target selection for violent acquisitive crimes (e.g. carjacking, drug robbery, etc.), many interviewees described looking for punks as targets, as they were soft and easy to victimize and, at least in the offender's mind, there was little to no chance that they would retaliate. In picking a carjacking target, C-Ball explained that not only did he like the car, but the driver, 'looked like a punk …

you know how like a fag, you [know] like [a] homosexual.' Rayray explained, 'I rob bitches, bitch ass fools that ain't gonna do nothing. I rob dudes that's weak, that's soft, they got a lot of money ... he ain't gonna do nothing.' Smokedog explained why he chose a given mark for a drug robbery:

Interviewer: Why was he such a mark?
Smokedog: Cause he a punk, man.
Interviewer: Can you explain that?
Smokedog: He soft. You know how you look [at] a person and you realize, man, that nigger soft man, that dude soft, man. That's how I looked at him like man, he soft, I'm taking that dope. I ain't buying that, I'm taking that. So I caught him and I took it like I said I was gonna.

Even maintaining the appearances of street masculinity by having money and underworld success wasn't enough to avoid the punk label. Describing his target selection for a drug robbery, Darnell explained why he selected the individual in this way: 'He was a motherfucker that had all of this dope and money but he was a bitch, real soft ... he was more like a little girl. He was the kind that did his feet and his hands, got his nails done ... personally, I thought he was gay.' Darnell strongly linked the notion of punk with femininity and sexuality here. Not only was the dealer's street toughness questioned and denigrated, his sexuality – an essential component of masculinity – was also made problematic.

In discussing how he chose targets, Kow provided a clear definition of 'punk', as well as showing how, in a shallow social interaction, such a determination can be made about a stranger:

Interviewer: How can it [the urge to pull a carjacking] hit you though? Does it hit you because the car is nice or does it hit you because the guy who was on the phone was weak or something?
Kow: All that, you know what I'm saying, all that, like a bitch.
Interviewer: Did he look like a bitch?
Kow: Yeah, all of that.
Interviewer: Why did he look like a bitch?
Kow: I don't know, it just something, he look like a bitch, just like we could whip him.

In a sense, then, a punk was anyone a given person thought he could 'take' in a violent altercation.

Similarly, how someone acted in the course of a robbery or assault could elicit the punk label. Looney Ass Nigger described, with clear condescension, the response of a carjacking victim:

> They crying, 'Please man, please, man', they kind of get on your nerves. You might want to smack them and tell them to shut up or something because that can mess with you head while you doing it. Crying, 'Oh, my momma' and all this, 'gonna miss me' and all that. Shut up, shut up and just get on the ground, let's get this over with.

Anderson (1999) described the street norms related to robbery in his ethnography of Germantown. While the core of the robbery event is a contest of wills, once a victim realized that the robber had gotten 'the jump' on them, they were to acquiesce to the robbery, playing their highly scripted role without resistance of fault. Here the problem is not failing to recognize the robber's power in the situation, but rather an excessive recognition of it. It is widely known on the streets that the violence inherent within an armed robbery event is a threat, not an actuality. While the core of a robbery is the robber's violent presentation of self, creating what Wright and Decker (1997) called 'the illusion of impending death', a streetwise man (or woman) should realize that it is just that: an illusion. If one's property is turned over it is understood that they will not be killed. The victim in the above incident displayed a lack of bravery and toughness in his collapse in the face of the carjacking.

Tall similarly described a viable target: 'He showed fear, I mean when a person shows fear then automatically, to me, I feel that, and he's automatically scared, so if I can use my strength ... by pulling him out of the car, 'cause he had already showed me fear in him ... he couldn't look me in the eye when I asked for change, then I knew I had him.' There were practical aspects to this technique of target selection. Individuals perceived as weaker were seen as less likely to retaliate and less likely to successfully resist a robbery attempt, yet the gendering of the behavior was clear in the language chosen to discuss the events. By feminizing the targets in their descriptions, the men established themselves as occupying an elevated position in the gender hierarchy of the streets.

Robbing a drug dealer typically precluded them from going back to that same dealer later as legitimate customers (see Jacobs 2000), but some interviewees mentioned doing just that – they were not afraid of retaliation due to the dealer's punk status. Loco described meeting on the street a drug dealer he had robbed the night before:

Loco:	The next day he [the victim] asked me where can he get his three hundred [dollars] and I told him I don't owe you three hundred [dollars] and walked out of his face. And to this day I buy weed … from him.
Interviewer:	You still buy weed from this guy?
Loco:	Yeah, and dope.
Interviewer:	So he's soft?
Loco:	Yeah, he's soft.

While Jacobs (2000) discussed that the threat of retaliation was central to the ways in which drug robbers managed robberies and their lives, Loco's lack of concern stemmed from the dealer's lack of appropriate response to his victimization. Following streetlife norms, the dealer should have exacted revenge on Loco. The fact that he continued to sell drugs to Loco further reinforced his status as a soft man, or a punk.

Punks as 'weak' men

Men who did not uphold the rules of violence on the street, especially those centered on retaliation, were also labeled punks. By not striking back at those who had wronged them, they failed to live up to the strict standards of hegemonic street masculinity about how and when violence should be used. It was not just that a man had to be violent and 'hold his square', there were norms of honor and respect that went along with it. It was not enough to just retaliate; a man had to retaliate in a certain fashion or face being labeled a punk. Chewy explained an incident in which he was attacked, but the offender kept his identity secret:

Interviewer:	That's kind of sneaky, isn't it?
Chewy:	Yeah … I think it's a punk move … that thing gay … it [is] something a bitch would do or something.
Interviewer:	A bitch would like playing all nice and then get you when you're –
Chewy:	Yeah, two-faced or something like that.
Interviewer:	When you are not expecting it.
Chewy:	Yeah.

Thus, a true test of manhood was to provide your opponent with a fighting chance to stand up to your violence. Again, note the use of strongly femininizing language to describe the assailant. The use of the terms 'gay' and 'bitch' exhibited the strongly gendered sense of the behavioral expectations. Black described a similar situation: 'He knew [it was not right], hitting me from behind. Look, I'll take a ass whipping. You want to whip my ass, that's cool. You want my ass, you want my ass. [But hitting me] from behind and I ain't even expecting ... you don't pull no shit like that.' Goldie also described a similar situation: 'He treat[ed] me like a punk ... Shot me and didn't want to be seen ... he could have come up to me [face-to-face], shot me or whatever.'

While some members in the samples described similar violent offenses, especially taking the element of surprise from their victim, many regarded this as unmanly, as if not giving the victim a 'fighting chance'. As both the violence and the language of gender used were ways of constructing street hierarchies, the labeling of men who got the drop on them as 'punks' or 'cowards' was a way to maintain masculine face during the interview event. When enacting violent revenge, it was practical to surprise the victim. However, when *you* are surprised, your own masculinity has been challenged – you were not being observant or alert enough. Thus, discussing the event during an interview, these men redefined it in an attempt to preserve and/or restore their own masculinity by denying hegemonic masculinity to their victimizer. It was not a failing of personal vigilance that produced the victimization, but a lack of the assailant's honor.

Similarly, men who denied involvement in an activity to avoid a violent encounter were punks; they were trying to avoid responding to a masculinity challenge by denying their original actions. Big Will described finally tracking down someone for retaliation: 'He denied it, he punked out ... He said, "That wasn't me, I swear it", like he was begging. "It wasn't me."' Buck described a similar response. After being robbed, he tracked down the man who victimized him. When confronted, the man started crying, '"Just don't shoot me, don't shoot me." I said, "I'm gonna kill you if you make one fucked up move. Give me that shit." So I put my hand down in his jock strap, pulled it [drugs and money] out, shook him down, shook his socks down, made him get out of the car on my side ... popped the hood of his trunk and threw him in there and drove off.'

Describing why he robbed drug dealers, Do Dirty explained that, 'Dope dealers are the most punk ass niggers in the world, they are chumps. They are like girls ... they will pay to keep they ass from going to the penitentiary ... They marks, they little chumps, they will pay somebody to kill you.' In their perceived unwillingness to take care of their own problems, the dealers were seen as easy prey and deserving targets on the streets. Real men took care of their own business, stood up to challenges themselves and took responsibility for their own actions.

Punks as failed men

'Punk' was also a cognitive category applied to specific types of individuals on the streets, particularly homeless men and drug addicts. When he discussed robbing drug addicts, Spanky bluntly explained why he wasn't worried about retaliation: 'Who cares? It's like taking candy from a kid you know, don't worry about a dope fiend.' Don Love expressed similar feelings when talking about an addict he had victimized: 'The motherfucker ain't worth two slices of bread all smashed together.' In describing an encounter with a homeless man, E expressed the clear disgust he held for such an individual. After being robbed by a homeless man, and acquiescing to the robbery, E described how he and his peers responded to the incident:

> I know how it feels to be broke, to be homeless. And my boys said, "do you want us to go find and kill him?" and I said "no", 'cause he gonna kill himself ... people like that gonna kill themselves ... Homeless guys don't mean it [robbery as an insult], there ain't no point in hurting him. People owe us money, living high, gotta make an example of them.

E was clear that he viewed the man with disdain and not as a real *man*, but that the injury was not worth responding to, since it was perpetrated by someone without street credibility. Thus, ironically, since the homeless man's status was well below E's, he did not need to reassert his own position, as his street credibility was not truly challenged.

Junebug, a crack user, described how he saw himself frequently treated by dealers:

> They think they better than the next motherfucker, man, you know because they think, dudes sell heroin, man, you know, like they gonna get a dude high off heroin but them little cats discriminate, the motherfuckers that smoke crack. 'Oh he just

an old crackhead motherfucker' ... what the motherfucker fails to realize is man, you know, we make you, you don't make us. Without us, your crack ain't shit 'cause you will still be stuck with that shit, you know ... They don't have no respect for the older dudes ... I'm not beggin' you for anything, I'm buying what I want from you, but I still got to be a crackhead motherfucker to you. But you a blunthead motherfucker 'cause you smoke blunts all day so you ain't no better than me. You fucking with a drug too.

Clearly Junebug saw this form of treatment as a challenge to his masculinity and used the interview to turn the tables on the dealers themselves, equating their use of marijuana with his use of crack cocaine. He also attempted to invert the dominant/subordinate relationship of dealer–addict by saying 'we make you, you don't make us'. Despite Junebug's discourse, street wisdom rarely equates the use of marijuana with that of crack. Especially as the crack epidemic wore on in major US cities, crack users were demonized not only by politicians and the mainstream media, but also within the very neighborhoods that crack dominated years before.

Overall, the label 'punk' emerged as the key subordinate masculinity used by men to define their own street masculinity. It was a label men used to denigrate and degrade other men, primarily for the purpose of raising their status. Men could become 'punks' for a number of reasons, all of which related to failures to uphold and enact the more hegemonic masculinity demands in streetlife social contexts.

Masculine capital

'Doing gender' required drawing upon a set of social and cultural capital. Many men in the sample used financial resources to project and proclaim their masculinity via conspicuous consumption. Through various displays of wealth, men could visually verify their ability to earn money and thereby establish their masculinity.

Flossing

'Flossing' involved public displays of financial capital. This took several forms, including blatantly displaying large amounts of money, wearing expensive, fashionable clothing, adding expensive features to a car (e.g. stereo systems, rims, curb feelers, etc.), and other flashy behavior. It also involved extravagant spending in a social context, primarily buying drugs and otherwise being involved in a culture of desperate partying (Shover and Henderson 1995; Shover and Honaker 1992; Wright and Decker 1994, 1997). Such behavior enhanced masculine capital on the streets by establishing financial success. Further, by carelessly or immoderately spending money, a man presented the image of someone who had easy access to cash whenever he wanted it.

Among the interviewees, such extravagance was frequently referred to as 'fucking the money' – spending it quickly and lavishly on non-essential items consumed in a party atmosphere. Little Rag's comments were typical: 'I truly fuck money up ... weed, clothes, shoes, shit like that, trims [sunglasses].' Loco explained how he spent the take from his illegal activity: 'I was buying weed, drinks, partying, hotels. I was going to the club ... We fucked the money ... getting high, buying shit, all type of stuff.' Binge said, 'I just blowed it [the money] man. With the $200, me and my girl, we went and did a bit of shopping ... but the money I got from the wallet I just blowed that, drinking, and smoking marijuana.' Looney Ass Nigger concurred, explaining that after a successful robbery he and his friends 'blew that [money] the same night ... on drinking and smoking, going out to eat, just chilling'.

Kow, responding to a question about how he spent the money from his crimes, said, 'Kicking it. Nothing special, just kicking it ... [My friends] ain't got to get no money, we just kicked it with the money ... wherever it came from it was all good.' Later in the interview, he continued, '[I] just got the money to blow, so fuck it, blow it ... whatever you see you get, fuck it. Spend that shit. It wasn't yours from the getty up [from the start], you know what I'm saying? You didn't have it from the jump so can't act like you careful with it, it wasn't yours to care ... It's just gone. You can go find a whore ... some shit like that, buy you some weed.' Smokedog spent his money this way, saying, 'I like to go out, kick it, I'm a party animal, I drink kegs all day everyday. ... That's how we kick it, we spends money ... then we fuck money up, we live tight man, we'll stay out late at night, get us some motherfucker and get that money right back.' Mo expressed a similar looseness of spending: 'Kept it ... get high, drunk ... I just blow money. Money is not something that is going to achieve for nobody ... so everyday there's not a promise so I just spend it.'

Clothes

Appearance was a critical part of presentation of self on the streets; men used clothing and jewelry to establish social position, especially as expensive clothing reflected a man's possession of large amounts of extra money. Icy Mike described how he dressed when going out to clubs: 'I had my gray snakeskin shoes, I had on my gray slacks and shit. I had on my gray, black and white sweater, chain on. Got my motherfucking golf hat on tipped to the side. I'm a pimp.'[5]

Bacca, like many others, specifically mentioned the desire to buy clothes as a motivating element of his violent crimes: 'I wanted Polo, I wanted new shoes.' Rayray explained that, 'a lot of young cats out here like to dress nice … like a Tommy Hilfinger shirt [sic]'. Lil Player offered a similar justification for his illegal activity: 'Just used to have the money to go buy me gear, whatever, shoes, clothes.' Smokedog explained what he did with the proceeds from a particularly lucrative drug robbery: 'I celebrated … I kicked it … clothes, shoes, everything. I got so much clothes I don't even know, man, I don't know what to do with it.'

Cars

Cars were also a central medium for conspicuous consumption on the streets. As with mainstream society, spending money on a vehicle and vehicle accessories was indicative of financial position. Playboy described the essential value of an expensive, 'tricked-out' car on the streets. 'Tricked out' was a street term that described a vehicle that had extensive, expensive modifications and additions. Raising or lowering the body, additional headlamps, stereos, new rims, window tinting and curb feelers were all common methods of tricking out a vehicle: 'The new Cadillac truck [SUV] … let's just say he puts a 20-inch rims on there with some bows. Tint the windows, you know, and just put some nice little rumble into it [stereo]. Somebody gonna look at this like, oh yeah, he got some money.' Others identified the same elements on vehicles as establishing greater levels of street credibility and gender capital. Tall mentioned, 'I like the rims, man. I like the Lincolns, the Cadillacs and 98's … I go for the Lincolns, but if I need something fast like a Firebird, it's just a fast life.' Snake described a car he found attractive and carjacked: 'It was light gray with white stripes at the back. It had 20-inch blades on it … and the beats [stereo], we liked the beats. He got tints on it.'

Lowdown clearly articulated the perceived link between driving a fancy car and neighborhood status: 'I'm gonna tell you. A dope dealer drive a car like a Suburban or rims and gold ... dressed up pretty nice and everything.' Tall made a further connection between cars and other elements of masculine street capital: 'I mean, that's what young guys thrill off of, a nice car, something to get around in ... A woman catcher ... yeah, I means cars what's happening for anyone.'

One important facet of having a vehicle was to gain masculine capital by being seen driving around the neighborhood. As C-Low explained:

> You got people you know that's driving around. We just wanna know how it feels. We're young and we ain't doing shit else. So they see you driving the car, they gonna say, "Hey, there's C-Low" and such and such. That makes us feel good cause we're riding and then when we're done riding we wreck the car or give it to somebody else and let him ride.

Little Tye explained it was just this sort of behavior that often triggered the urge to jack a car: 'Shit. Saw a little Cad [Cadillac] riding one o'clock in the morning with his gal over there, pumping his beats, riding his rims, goddamn me and my partner got on [committed the carjacking].' Sleezee-E described what he did after a carjacking: 'Yeah, we drove it around through the hood, showing it off ... did a little flossing.' Binge behaved similarly:

> I was just riding around listening to music, picked up a couple of friends of mine. We rode around ... I was chilling, you know. I was driving alone with the music playing up loud. Ha ha. You know, I wasn't even worried about whether you got the car or not, you know ... I was just feeling good 'cause I'm not use to driving that much you know, 'cause I don't have a car ... that's why I do a carjacking ... I just play it off to the tee, run all the gas off, keep the sounds up as loud as I can, keep the heat on, you know, just abuse the car, you know.

Binge's comments were especially interesting in the over-the-top use and abuse he would visit on a jacked car just to earn masculine capital on the streets. Parallel to 'fucking the money', since the car wasn't his and it came to him easily, why bother to take care of it? The abuse of the car broadcast his ability to get another one whenever he wanted it.

Many of the men also discussed keeping parts off the cars they jacked to put on their own vehicles. Describing the take from a carjacking, Little Tye explained, 'My partner, he wanted some rims. He had just bought this Malibu and he just wanted rims. I needed a radio and some speakers.' Accordingly, they jacked a car to get those specific items. In such cases, the primary motivation for the carjacking was the enhancement of masculinity capital on the streets – not through a reputation of toughness or dangerousness, but via the display of wealth.

Women

Another source of masculine capital on the streets was being seen with or having a reputation for being seen with women in the neighborhood. While other aspects of male–female interaction in the streets will be covered later, it is worth exploring here how many men saw women as a masculinity-enhancing accoutrement. In addition to the above description of 'fucking the money', when asked how they spent the illegal gains of their criminal activity, many men directly mentioned using the money to gain female companionship. C-Ball simply said that in his circle of offenders, 'everybody go to the East Side [across the Mississippi River in Illinois] to go see girls and stuff, you know, meet girls.' Tall's response was similar: 'Spend it on? Having a nice time, women, I mean whatever there at the moment.' V-O's response was just as simple, 'We just laugh, kick back, go find a couple of girls, chill.' His response firmly united the search for women with broader 'fucking the money' behaviors. Smooth G made the additional connection of flossing cars to attract women: 'That [is] they way they do it if they [are] flashing [flossing]. It will bring women toward them. Somebody see you with two TVs in your truck they gonna be like, you got some money.' The objectification of women here was strong. Many of the men in the interviews analyzed for this study placed women in the same broad category of 'flossing' possessions with cars, jewelry and clothes. They were typically described as an accoutrement to the 'life as party' lifestyle.

Conclusion

As explored here, there were many facets to masculinities on the streets of Saint Louis. While some of these elements parallel those of mainstream masculinities, most aspects were intensified and attended to more strongly. For example, while all men tend toward presentations of self that emphasize independence and self-sufficiency, in this sample this self-imposed social isolation was often phrased in the language of survival. Taken as a whole, these elements of hegemonic street masculinity reinforced the connections between maleness and the use of violence on the streets of Saint Louis. The need to establish and maintain a reputation as a man in the neighborhoods explored here clearly generated inclinations toward violence among the interviewees. The vast majority of the men here saw actual or potential violence as omnipresent on the streets and they constructed their actions and presentations of self in such a fashion as to be vigilant toward and capable of dealing with any challenges that arose in their daily interactions.

The relationship between gender and violence was mutually reinforcing. While the demands of masculinity as outlined here clearly established violence as a behavioral expectation, the form street masculinity took – especially the emphasis on not trusting others and the overpowering fatalism – was strongly influenced by the potentiality of violence emerging out of even the shallowest social interactions. This dialect of masculinity and violence further generated situational role strain in the accomplishment of masculinity. Men on the streets of Saint Louis often were forced to choose between behaviors that are broadly defined as masculine (independent, toughness, being forthright in a violent confrontation) and behaviors that were eminently practical, but less masculine (e.g. accepting assistance in a retaliation, using sneakiness to get the drop on someone in an ongoing dispute – behaviors that were typically defined as 'punk' behaviors in the sample). These inherent contradictions of street masculinity emphasized not only the dynamic nature of gender but also the nuances inherent in even hegemonic gender performances.

The norms of street masculinity reinforced the alienation felt by the interviewees here; additionally, the social distance experienced by the men was widened by their commitment to this specific form of masculinity. The emphasis on independence and violence accentuated an already tenuous relationship with mainstream institutions. As shown in the discussions of work, men embedded in streetlife experienced multiple disinclinations toward legitimate work. When they gained such employment, they brought with them to the workplace the interactional norms of the street that enhanced the pre-existing negative perceptions of blue collar work. The ultimate failures experienced in that social realm further marginalized participation in mainstream social life and reinforced attachment and commitment to streetlife norms.

Compared with prior work on masculinity and violence in youth gangs, the older men here expressed stronger inclinations toward working alone and maintaining individuality at all costs. Although gang research has emphasized the bonds between gang members, the men here often discussed their desire to be unattached and uninvolved with others, both in offending behaviors and broader social arenas. Because these issues were not probed in the interviews, it is difficult to explain exactly why this shift occurred. It could be attributed to growing up in social networks later fragmented by 'aging out' and incarceration. It could also be a product of experiencing numerous double-crosses over the years.

Primarily, mainstream masculine norms (e.g. independence, toughness and self-sufficiency) and aspirations (e.g. attainment of status via income and wealth) were refracted in the prism of streetlife as it has developed in a heavily disadvantaged community. The broader gender capital (e.g. mainstream work and education) forming the core of American masculinity was generally unavailable to the men in this sample. Thus, street masculinity derived more from the capital available to them (potential and real violence), as well as from participation in the underground economy that provided the financial resources crucial for masculinity performances.

The next chapter focuses on the ways in which these elements of masculinity were transformed into a street reputation and how issues of building and maintaining a reputation guided masculinity challenges. It explores why most men on the street see violence as a desirable, if not required, response to such interactions.

Notes

1 The female street names were similarly gendered, though they fell into two broad categories. Many offered up clearly feminized names (e.g. Lady Bug, Baby Doll, Pooh Bear, Peaches, Pumpkin, Sugar), while others offered up names closer to those the men (e.g. Nasty Bitch and Lady Ice).

2 Homies: friends and associates, short for 'homeboy' or 'homegirl'.

3 Interviewees in the sample commonly referred to a colostomy bag as a 'shit bag'.

4 In other interviews, Smokedog interjected himself into the conversation, sometimes when directly asked a question by the interviewee, other times just chiming in with his take on the event being discussed.

5   In fact, based on discussions elsewhere in the interview, Icy Mike does appear to be a pimp. However, it should be noted that the terms 'pimp' and 'pimping' do not always literally refer to controlling a stable of women involved in sex work. In some contexts, pimp simply refers to someone engaged in extravagant conspicuous consumption.

Chapter 4

Every motherfucker gonna try to punk you: masculinity challenges

The previous chapter explored the key elements and behavioral demands of street masculinity within Saint Louis' streetlife. This chapter focuses on how the demands of these situated gender roles generated and perpetuated violence. This occurred primarily through the perceived need to respond to masculinity challenges with varying degrees of force. The demands of street masculinity centralized the role of violence in the creation of a street reputation through either establishing masculinity by challenging someone else or defending against the challenges of another. These masculinity challenges formed the core instigation of much interpersonal street violence.

Whereas there were indeed practical elements to these norms of violence, the interviewees clearly linked an ability to build and maintain a reputation to masculinity. Men who could achieve and activate strong street reputations for violence found their masculinity capital enhanced; those who failed tests on the streets not only found themselves targets for future victimization, but assigned to subordinate masculinities by associates and peers. This chapter discusses the interviewee's perceptions of the importance of building and maintaining a street reputation and then explores the many forms of masculinity challenges. Finally, it examines why the vast majority of men in the sample see no other way to respond to these interactions save with violence.

The importance of reputation

Almost every interviewee emphasized that one of the most valuable
– if not the most valuable – asset a man possessed on the streets
was a strong reputation. The more widely known you were in the
community, the easier it was to go about your daily life. Reputation
also facilitated criminal and non-criminal actions. This was clearly
evident in the following exchange:

Interviewer: You've got to have a rep on the streets as a gangster, I
mean …

Slim: I got that … they see me coming a mile away, the people
that see me coming a mile away, they know me. They
know who I will rob and who I won't rob. I'm out there
but, I mean, that don't mean because you know me and
I know you as long as I been knowing you, see there is
one thing I don't do. I don't rob my friends, I do not
do that. That's where that taboo comes in at … someone
strange, I got to have him … And I find out you got
some of that and don't nobody know nothing about it,
well I'll ask [about] him myself … and don't nobody
know nothing about him, I'm gonna get him.

In this case, Slim's reputation served to facilitate interactions with
street peers by reducing concerns whether he would victimize them.
By being known as someone who would not rob a friend, Slim
avoided some potentially violent encounters with street associates
who otherwise might have felt the need for proactive victimization.
Additionally, Slim discussed checking up on the target's reputation.
With no reputation or social network connections to dissuade him,
Slim saw the man as a target he could easily victimize.

As reputation is most frequently passed via word of mouth
around social networks, someone with a strong reputation in one
neighborhood or group might be unknown in another. Biddle noted
that reputation was often geographically tied: 'I got a rep in my
'hood you know. Now, outside my 'hood I get fucked up. I can't lie.'
A new arrival to a neighborhood not only faced many challenges to
test his mettle (see also Anderson 1999), but also needed to initiate
challenges to establish a position in the local hierarchy. This aspect
of reputation took on additional significance because of the nomadic
nature of men in the sample (see also Wright and Decker 1994). Few

men stayed in one place for very long and they found themselves constantly working to establish a street reputation.

Whereas the primary source of reputation was personal actions, the actions and reputations of your street associates could build up or tear down your own standing. Don Love explained this interconnection:

Don Love: Man, check this out. Most people afraid of me just by my conversation, you know what I'm saying?
Interviewer: What do you mean?
Don Love: Just by the way I talk and the way I move and the people I move with ... like you got a range of ... different people you deal with ... You don't deal with ignorance. You don't deal with stupidity. You don't deal with that 'cause if you deal with that then ... the motherfucker acts like you is a stupid, ignorant motherfucker.

Later in the interview, Don Love discussed how people responded to men with a strong reputation on the streets: 'When people walk, when we go in a club we hit the club and the niggers looking like [they] don't want to fuck with them guys there.' Through his own actions and the savvy selection of street peers, Don Love created an image that deterred challenges. D-Boy also discussed the advantages of a strong street reputation: 'Most people that see me they know that back in the day I did a lot of shit, so [they] don't fuck with me [now] ... I don't have to do shit now. I'm respected ... there's motherfuckers that still remember the shit I did.' Although valuable, community memory of D-Boy's prior actions also could have led to future altercations; that was the inherent contradiction of reputation. You gain capital when people were aware of your exploits, yet this process typically motivates the disrespected individual to seek retaliation. It also established you as a potential target for someone seeking to build a reputation of his own.

As with many elements of manhood, one's reputation must constantly be established. Partially due to a limited flow of information on the streets, no matter how well you broadcast your status, not everyone will be aware of your past exploits. Also, someone who has a strong reputation might be targeted by others who are looking to enhance their own reputation. A successful fight against someone with a strong reputation was one of the strongest enhancers of one's 'juice' on the streets. Black indicated that even though he had an established street reputation, this did not prevent other people from testing him:

Like I said I got my stature. Motherfuckers know, you know, what's up with me. Motherfuckers know, you know, I ain't no punk ... Motherfucker try anybody, you know, and motherfucker from out there we constantly try each other, you know what I'm saying? This motherfucker ain't got it. You hear them and like I told you some shit. It wasn't probably purposely getting into it like that ... Motherfuckers, that's what I said, motherfuckers around there will try you two, three times a day. They don't give a fuck, man. Look, man, they don't give a fuck, and you know 'cause to them it's about this hard shit.

This excerpt describes the powerful focus of building a reputation for violence that drove some men. A life framed by dedication to 'hard shit' led to violent encounter after violent encounter. Despite his attempt to dismiss such men as 'motherfuckers' who fatalistically simply 'don't give a fuck', his own behavior was strongly molded by these violent counters. Even though Black claimed that he tried to avoid these encounters, he never failed to respond in kind once challenged. Additionally, elsewhere in his interview he described savagely beating one of his associates with a lead pipe because the man had taken some of Black's marijuana (see later in this chapter for a thorough discussion of this episode).

The true value of a reputation rests within the enhanced masculine capital associated with it. Reminding people of who they are allows men on the streets to shape social interactions to better achieve their goals. The following excerpt shows how Goldie asserted his reputation as a form of social capital during an interaction. He described a discussion he had on the streets with the younger brother of a man who had shot him and who Goldie was trying to track down for revenge:

'Where's your brother at?' [I asked him]. 'I don't know where he is', [the brother said]. [So] I'm like, 'Well tell him Goldie, he's gonna holler at him about something.' Instantly he already knew, I could see that in his face that he already knew. 'So you're Goldie? OK, well, I'll tell him, I'll tell him.' I'm like, 'Are you shocked or what?'

Calling upon his reputation, Goldie not only put the younger brother on edge, but broadcast to the community that he was looking for the man who had injured him earlier. This reinforced Goldie's reputation, as the very act of seeking revenge on the streets established Goldie's masculine capital as someone not to be messed with.

Reputation was essential in that it established a power hierarchy on the streets. Men described constantly testing and struggling with each other for masculine and other social resources; knowing how you related to others was critical in determining how to interact with them, how to approach them, and most importantly, whether you could get over on them. Spanky explained:

> Let me tell you something about the 'hood. Everybody, it's always one main man in the hood that everybody know, you see what I'm saying, one main person that everybody gonna know ... like I say face, a man's face, everybody know [his] face ... everybody know him ... 'cause he usually the cat [that has done] the most stuff that standout ... he's the one that's turning ... he's just known, I'll put it like that, everybody knows him.

Red drew a parallel between age and the hierarchy of the streets; just as there were differences between children and adults, there were differences between *real* street men and others:

> See, you know what, a lot of people that knows me, know not to play with me. I tell people off the top: if I want to play, I got kids. I go home and play with my kids. If I want to play, I got a nephew. I'll go play with my nephew. I got a seven-, eight-year-old nephew staying at my mamma's house. I go play with them if I want to play. Life is serious with me. Life is too short and I ain't gonna let nobody in their right mind take me out of my life, not right now, you know? ... Don't mess with me and I ain't gonna mess with you.

There were several layers to Red's discourse. Primarily, he emphasized that many younger men on the streets did not take threats of violence seriously. Older men discussed how younger men – whom they often referred to as boys, emphasizing the nature of age grading on the streets – frequently displayed firearms, but did not seem prepared to use them. Such actions were seen as stupid by the older, street-embedded men, who interpreted drawing a weapon as one of the strongest masculinity challenges on the streets. If a weapon was drawn, many men insisted, you had better be ready to use it then and there. If you didn't, the person facing the weapon would either draw his own weapon – and use it – or come back armed later.

Tensions in establishing reputation

On the streets you must establish your 'juice' – something easily fulfilled through criminal activity (see Katz 1988; Anderson 1999). Lafonz explained:

> You know, you do sometimes talk like that [bragging about one's criminal accomplishments] just to let people know that you are in a certain situation ... if you're around certain people and that subject get brought up ... it's like, yeah, I beat ass ... I done beat this many asses ... everybody gotta kind of pronounce their manhood ... I beat ass and I can prove it. You know what I'm saying? ... That happen a lot.

A few minutes later in the interview, Lafonz not only indicated why having a reputation was essential, but also explained how the hierarchy of the streets worked within groups of peers and street associates:

> They [friends or peers] might not give you as much respect [if you do not have a reputation for violence]. They might not beat your ass or nothing, but they'll probably, like, do you wrong. You know, like, make you put, like, buy all their weed or something, you know, just treat you like a bitch, make you run to the store, do all type of little gopher type shit, little punk shit ... just be like the little peon.[1] 'We'll just do him how we want to', you know. Talk bad about him.

In the competitive hierarchy of the streets, men not only had to worry about how strangers and former victims approached them, they also had to be wary of how their street peers interpreted their reputation. The following exchange with Junebug highlighted a central tension inherent in reputation-building: walking the fine line between establishing yourself as someone with street credibility and letting too many specific pieces of information get out about your criminal actions:

Interviewer: Did you brag about it [a robbery] to all your friends?
Junebug: Oh no. I just tell them who did it and the killing and shit you did, you know ... I told my friends. We sit up, and kick up. Got high.
Interviewer: Do you normally tell people afterwards?

Junebug: Yes. Just people I'm cool with. Not anyone … I don't brag about it, you know … .It don't make no sense to brag about it because, see, you could be bragging and ain't no telling this might be somebody's cousin or relative, anybody, you see what I'm saying?

Men on the streets constantly negotiated the fine line of building and maintaining a reputation by 'broadcasting' their manhood without divulging too much information about the specifics of their actions. When that happened, former victims, their friends and relatives, or the police would learn enough about the person's actions to place his freedom and physical well-being in jeopardy.

Sources of masculinity challenges

There were numerous violence triggers on the streets; perceived and actual slights as well as potential and realized victimization all demanded some form of response to avoid the loss of masculine and street reputation credentials. Some of the men in the sample were extremely sensitive to threats; the most minor provocations elicited violent reprisals. Most seemed willing to let minor slights slide (unless there was a history between the individuals involved), but few would, or could, in their minds, ignore more serious threats to themselves, their families, or even close peers. The norms of street masculinity clearly dictated the need to 'hold one's square' and respond when challenged.

Minor slights

Some of the men reported seeing the most minor incidents as slights against them and their masculinity and requiring a violent response. From being looked at 'wrong' to being accidentally jostled in a public place, these seemingly innocuous interactional *faux pas* generated incidents of serious violence. TC described a violent incident in which the victim's provocation was minimal at best. Earlier in the day, TC's car had been vandalized; he described how he chose an essentially random target in a grocery store to unleash his frustration and anger:

It just so happened that later on that day somebody had pissed me off by doing something, you know, bumped me or something

83

... he bumped me, I was just pissed ... he just walked past me. He bumped me and I just snapped. I turned him around and hit him with the right, hit him with the left, and then I grabbed him and ... I slammed his face into the freezer window.

Dub described how similar, unintentional contact could generate violence: 'We all went to the club ... people bumped into people ... I got kicked out of the club 'cause I was starting [to] fight [over the incidental contact] ... a little while later the dude [whom Dub fought with] got kicked out of the club.' Dub had been waiting outside for the man to exit, and when he did the two fought in the parking lot to settle what they both perceived as an affront to their reputations.

Not surprisingly, bars were the site of numerous incidents where violence emerged from minor slights. Though alcohol played some role in these incidents, clubs and bars were social arenas where individuals established reputations and masculine capital in front of others. These witnesses could intensify an individual's perception of the seriousness of a slight or challenge and catalyze a more violent response. Red described an incident in a tavern where he accidentally bumped someone.

I had an incident you know like when this dude, we was in the tavern ... [a]nd you know in the tavern you gotta, it's just friends, for instance you in a tavern, you gota a nice lady, but everybody gonna complement your lady. Well see at the time the dude and his girlfriend they was going through a little spat ... I just happened to walk over there by and then when I walked I made a mistake and like tripped a little bit, you know, and [I] spilt my drink on him ... he just got up and knocked the shit out of me ... for spilling my drink all over him ... I ain't never seen this dude a day in my life ... he didn't give me no time to say sorry ... he just smacked me ... open hand. He just put me up a handprint in my face ... everyone was watching so I feel kind of bad ... he never should have put his hands on me ... He made me look bad.

This encounter was highly problematic for both men in involved; they are both in a strongly front-stage environment (Goffman 1955, 1959). The man whom Red spilled his drink on was clearly agitated by his conflict with the woman, a conflict potentially being overheard by others in his immediate vicinity. In and of itself this was a test of the man's masculinity due to the strong street-emphasis on controlling women. The man's immediate smacking of Red places Red in a challenge situation. The ensuing exchange between Red and the interviewer established Red's perspective on the inherent masculinity challenge underpinning the incident.

Interviewer: Why is that in your mind? Were you drinking or smoking [marijuana]?

Red: I had just had one little drink.

Interviewer: And you spilled part of it.

Red: Yeah. But you know like I say, a man don't never put his hand on another man, you know. You're supposed … look, man, he ain't gonna give me time enough to say, 'Look, man, I'm sorry.'

Interviewer: He didn't give you time to say you were sorry.

Red: Right. I tripped. I'm sorry. [I would have said] 'Whatever it cost I will pay for it, you know. I'll give you some money, man, to pay for your shirt.'

Interviewer: What kind of drink was it?

Red: I had a shot of Cognac.

Interviewer: Oh, so that would stain. Yeah.

Red: Yeah. Like I say, in my mind I know I'm gonna go on and do this here [exact revenge] cause I ain't never in my life had a motherfucker smack me before. Beside my mom and my dad. Them are the only one I ever had in my life smack me.

In his mind, this was an emasculating slight that Red could not allow to go without a response. The public nature of the encounter is crucial. Not only was Red hit in front of other people, the manner in which he was struck – an open-handed slap on the face – was a serious masculinity challenge. That is how one strikes a woman. Red's reaction was not limited to being hit; he also responded to being feminized in front of the other bar patrons. The following exchange explored what happened after Red was hit.

Interviewer: OK, so right after he hit you, you walked out the door?

Red: Right.

Interviewer: Why did you walk out?

Red: Because I was gonna get him. I was gonna kill him. I straight up was gonna kill him … You know, because he

	never should have put his hands on me … I'm sitting out there. I'm waiting on him to come out the bar. So 12 o'clock passes and he ain't there. He don't come out … I waited out there for almost like four or five hours and then the dude come out.
Interviewer:	Oh, that long?
Red:	Yeah, cause I made it by like nine. The bar don't close till about 1:30.
Interviewer:	OK so a few hours you waited …
Red:	I waited all that time on that dude … So about 1:15 he comes out. He comes and gets ready to get in his car … So when I seen them come out the bar already in my mind I got in my mind the state of my mind, I'm gonna kill this man.
Interviewer:	OK, so you're sitting in your car. There's other people coming out this whole time. He doesn't come out.
Red:	He doesn't come out until it's almost time for the bar to close … his date done left … I seen her when she got in the cab … So he comes out and he walks to his car and I walks up behind him, right … He don't see me. So when he decide to get into his car, like he going to his car – soon as he unlocked his car and get ready to get in his car I hit him about seven times on the back of the head.
Interviewer:	With the gun?
Red:	With the gun. I'm shooting him.
Interviewer:	How close were you when you …
Red:	Oh, about this close [indicating the distance between the interviewer and the interviewee – a few feet].
Interviewer:	Did he see you?
Red:	He should have seen me. Yeah, yeah, he seen me.
Interviewer:	So, wow, that's a pretty serious, another serious response.
Red:	Yes. But see look, when you see, OK, when you coming out – I mean it's like when you coming out – you just been out. You enjoying yourself, you're partying, you forget about what you did to a person. But you also got to know when you walk out that door you better watch your back … [so], I snuck up behind him.
Interviewer:	Wouldn't you want to confront the guy in front of his face like you, you slapped me. Nobody slaps me, you're gonna pay.

Red: No, see what you do is when you do stuff like that there, to give option of time to break back into the car. Either he can get a chance to break out and start running. When you sneak up behind him and you hit him once, 'bang', he gonna spin around. So when he spin around he gonna see you.

Interviewer: Where'd you aim that first shot at?

Red: In the back of the head ...

Interviewer: A lot of guys, you know, they want that satisfaction of this guy seeing you do it.

Red: But see, you know what? You gonna have the satisfaction ... you hit him one time, you see, and the reaction is so tough the way you hit him once they gonna spin around ... they gonna see you ... off the top the first thing he's gonna say always is: 'Awww – that's it' ... and when he said 'Aww', [so I say] 'Awe yeah, remember me', boom, boom, boom. 'You remember me?' Boom. Just like that and that's it.

Red's narrative showed not just how a minor incident catalyzed violence that then led to lethal violence, but also how the public nature of the conflict spurred the desire for serious payback. Note how Red responded once the interview began to probe and test the 'masculinity' of the technique used to kill the man. Once Red has described the executioner-style slaying, the interviewer suggests that other men would want the person to know who killed them. Caught in a situation where his manhood is being questioned, Red began to explain how the victim would have been aware of Red's identity before he died.

Being talked down to

Many men in the sample discussed taking offense at the way they were spoken to during social interactions. When not given the respect or deference they felt they deserved, certain interviewees saw this as a slight worthy of violent retribution. Dub straightforwardly explained: 'If you get smart with me I won't put my hands on you, but I'll let you know you can't talk with me any way you want to. You got to respect me if I respect you. If I can't respect you then you can disrespect me.' Dub indicated that in any street interaction he demanded a certain level of respect. Other men identified specific social situations in which respect was denied and how that translated directly into violence when the expected esteem was not provided.

Lowdown, in describing how he selected a particular drug dealer as a target for a robbery, explained how the dealer's refusal of credit to him was taken as a challenge: 'I just sit down and think about, OK, so he got all this and then he gonna talk down to me like that? OK, I consider you to be a player hater ... because he looking down on me. So I just target people like that.' While the response was not immediate – the retaliatory robbery took place later that night – the earlier insult was a clear motivation for the selection of that specific dealer as a target. Bacca experienced a similar interaction with a street dealer:

Interviewer: So you asked him for [the drugs on credit] and he said, 'Get out of my face?'

Bacca: He told me that, that really made me mad right there. That didn't make me only want to rob him, it made me want to kill him ... He was just acting and I didn't like the way he was acting.

Moon also described being spoken down to by a drug dealer:

Interviewer: And he started talking to you like –
Moon: Like I'm a lost boy.
Interviewer: Talking down to you?
Moon: Exactly ... it's an insult, I don't play games.

The insult was clear; Moon felt like he was being treated like a child. He was not given the respect he felt he deserved as a man – both due to age and street reputation. As with Lowdown and Bacca, a violent armed robbery was how Moon chose to re-establish his masculinity. Not only did the robbery fulfill the drug user's other needs – free drugs and additional cash to spend – it also reasserted his perceived position in the street hierarchy.

Others discussed how daily interactions and recreation in the community could provoke violence if proper respect was not given to others. Kow described an incident in which he wasn't directly insulted or challenged, but felt compelled to respond with violence nonetheless:

It was a basketball game ... little guy was talking shit ... actually he talked about a friend of mine, for real. Man, I don't want nothing to do with that ... he started popping, 'I'm gonna do this and I'm gonna do that', and I hit him ... He talked to me like he wanted to do it to me so I punched him ... he was talking shit at me and I'm telling him that I don't want to hear it.

Lafonz similarly described how a pick-up basketball game got out of hand and turned into fisticuffs over a minor slight:

We all hoping [playing basketball] and it was two of the little guys. The younger brother started mouthing off with this other guy 'cause of a bad call or something. But then it was like, 'You're a bitch, you soft', and the dude was like, 'You're not gonna call me a bitch no more. I'll beat your ass.' Then the dude was too big to be fighting them, for real. So his brother came in but he's still too small too ... so they just kept on. They just wouldn't stop.

The verbal altercation escalated when a participant's masculinity was questioned. The larger man felt he had to respond to being feminized ('You're a bitch, you soft'), a challenge made stronger by the fact that his insulter was smaller and younger than him. In the language of the streets, he has been 'dised', or disrespected and must reassert his position. Eventually they came to blows and Lafonz stepped in to help the smaller guys in the fight. To do otherwise, he felt, would jeopardize his own reputation. He continued:

It was like it'd have made me look bad ... 'cause like they not my for real partners but we from the same neighborhood and if I sit there and let these two grown-ass men beat these two little dudes' ass that's gonna look bad on me. ... It's like I can't let you get beat up and just sit there and watch it ... that'd be a bitch move ... just if me and you buddies and we go out one night and you happen to get into it with somebody at the bar and they just start beating your ass and I don't do nothing, that's be pretty fucked up if I just let you get your ass beat.

Thus, in order to avoid potentially being labeled as a punk, Lafonz got involved in a fight he saw as meaningless and originally tried to prevent. His action was propelled by his perception that he would be held to blame for the younger guys getting beaten up; part of street chivalry as it existed in the interviews was a broad perception that a real man would protect people who were being unfairly challenged. This responsibility was further enhanced by the fact that the smaller men were from his neighborhood – a frequently mentioned line of allegiance whether one was involved in neighborhood-based gang behavior or not. Again, the masculine qualities on the line in the situation are made even clearer by the language used. Lafonz lamented that to stand by and watch the fight unfold would 'be a bitch move'. To protect his own reputation, he felt he had to enter into the brawl.

As discussed in Chapter 3, being labeled a crackhead was a way in which masculinity and respect were denied to people on the streets. This was not a derogation that many of the men in the sample accepted readily, however. Junebug, interviewed during the drug robbery project, claimed that crack dealers were his favorite robbery targets because of the constant disrespect he felt aimed at him from them. When asked why he specifically targeted street-level crack dealers, he explained:

> [I] like getting these cats man because they think they better than the next motherfucker man you know because they think, dudes sell heroin man, you know, like they gonna get a dude get high off of heroin but them little cats discriminate the motherfuckers that smoke crack. 'Oh he just an old crackhead motherfucker', you see what I'm saying you know. But what the motherfucker fails to realize is man, you know, we make you, you don't make us. Without us your crack ain't shit 'cause you will still be stuck with that shit you know. So I prefer to get the crack dealers because the majority of them be cats, you know, they don't have no respect for the older dudes you know. Because you know, I'm not begging you for anything, I'm buying what I want from you but I still got to be a crackhead motherfucker to you. But you a blunthead motherfucker 'cause you smoke blunts all day so you ain't no better than me. You fucking with a drug too.

In an attempt to circumvent the label of drug addict and the loss of control and self-empowerment (and thereby manhood) that it implies, Junebug attempted to invert the power hierarchies ('we make you') and then emphasized that as he was paying and not begging, he was still engaged in masculine behavior.

Later in the interview, Junebug described his response to a specific instance where someone treated him as an addict instead of a man:

I hit him in the head and bust his motherfucking head with a pistol. I like shit like that … man, you know this little nigger, the old punk ass nigger, he called me a motherfucking goddamn crackhead … I'm just another crackhead to his motherfucking ass but he got the nerve to beg for his motherfucking life … so it's fun to me.

Junebug's anger was clear, as was his almost sensual satisfaction (see Katz 1988) in establishing himself through violence as dominant over the dealer who had demeaned him. Lewis described a situation with a similar resolution. Lewis had approached a heroin dealer he bought from every few weeks, but he was five dollars short of the $50 he needed for the bag. The dealer rejected the sale at that point: 'He [the drug dealer] wanted to talk to [me] like [I] was a drug addict, you know, and I felt like he couldn't talk to me like that kind of way, like I'm a drug addict. If I'm a user, I'm a user, you know. So he took my money and balled it up and threw it in my face.' In response, Lewis robbed the dealer, employing more violence than necessary to accomplish the stick-up, thereby using that additional force to re-establish his own reputation on the streets.

Lowdown discussed a random encounter in a parking lot with a dealer he knew. This incident showed how even a chance meeting could produce slights that were perceived as serious and required violent responses. The dealer, upon seeing Lowdown, said, 'Oh man, you looking bad. You still on drugs and stuff like that?' Elaborating, Lowdown said, 'Yeah, you know. So I kind of took that personal … why do you look down on me when you probably done things wrong?' Later in the week, Lowdown robbed the dealer, going to his house to accomplish the crime.

Men used violence to re-establish themselves in the street hierarchy when another's labeling of them into a devalued status threatened their own position. In these examples, the men were not in a highly public space with many spectators. The affront to the offender's masculinity was not registered through the responses of observers to the action, but internally. Challenges occurring in public spaces with numerous witnesses (e.g. in taverns) provoked a strong perceived need to respond, with face-saving a driving force; yet unobserved challenges to a man's internalized sense of position also catalyzed violence.

Challenges over women

Many of the men in the sample discussed violent incidents that occurred over women. However, few mentioned initiating such confrontations. Most likely, this is due to the widespread view that women are not worth risking oneself over (see Chapter 5 for a full discussion of men's views of women). When men did mention being spurred to violence because they felt someone was homing in on their women, the violence was not framed with direct reference to the women. Rather, the interviewees highlighted the attitudes of men they eventually victimized. Icy Mike's description is typical:

> We was at the club. Motherfucker was trying to haul out with one of my little bitches. I don't give a fuck about the bitch 'cause I got somebody at home, it don't even matter, but the thing is this old boy is trying to holler at the bitch and then he want to try and throw it in my face. Like 'I'm on this bitch, what you gonna do about it?' … 'I don't give a fuck about her, you can fuck her.' But he's getting too high with this shit, he's feeling too confident with himself.

Icy Mike made it explicit that he had no attachment or investment with the woman in question – in fact, such an investment would be unmasculine. Rather, it was the attitude displayed by the other man that Icy Mike said triggered the violence.

Most of the offenders discussed being on the other side of these exchanges, being approached and challenged because they were hitting on someone else's woman. Biddle described a retaliation he received for such behavior: 'Well, they wrecked my car and tore my car up, like, came and just beat it up … I think because I was hitting [having sex with] one of his gals … his girlfriend.' Black described a similar situation: 'I was talking about his sister … She a freak[2] or whatever … everybody is with her … It was bothering him. So he took a little swing at me and he hit me from behind and shit … and when he did that he came up from behind. You know that's some cowardly shit. I gotta get that back [by retaliating].'

Speezy found himself confronted by 'some guy telling me about talking to his lady or whatever and all that. [I] told him it wasn't like that. [He] came up to me again, threatening me, telling me not to talk to his girl so I ain't messing around like that, I'm just talking to her. Next thing I know, he's pushing me … We got to fighting, fighting on the ground, scrambling this and that.' Chewy had a similar encounter: 'That's when her boyfriend walked up and said "What [are you] doing talking to my wife?" I'm like, "Man, I ain't know. I didn't even know you all was with them." I'm straight, you know. He started talking noise … I ain't … talking no noise with him. I've got a real quick temper and I just upped [hit] him.'

The frequency of men's descriptions of being challenged over women they were 'trying to get with' suggested that they had played both roles in the interaction with some frequency. However, due to the demands of street masculinity, they seemed to downplay their own initiations of such events. Such situations displayed their connectedness or investment in other people, something that ran distinctly counter to male ideals of independence. While misogynistic values found on the streets may have emphasized possession and 'ownership' of women, there were also powerful norms demanding that men downplay the amount of social and psycho-emotional energy they invested in sexual-romantic relationships. Admitting to starting a fight over a woman – especially a fight that may have potentially lethal consequences – violated key perceptions of common sense and 'appropriate' levels of attachment to and investment in women.

Flossing

As discussed in Chapter 3, conspicuous displays of wealth and income on the streets – especially their ability to obtain and extravagantly spend financial capital – were key ways that men established masculinity. This 'flossing' was seen as essential to establishing and maintaining one's reputation on the streets. However, this behavior was often perceived by others as an invitation to victimization. Buck explained: 'Some of them young guys, you got dudes 19, 20, 22 years old handling thousands of dollars. He gets an arrogant way about him. Kind of sassy and floss and shit you know. Those are the ones I normally target.' Do Dirty offered a similar explanation for how he selected robbery victims:

They be all standing outside … on the corner, flashing they little money in front of the little gals, counting they money, you know. They holler at they friends … That's a mark. You riding down the street, ain't got no money but you got a pistol and these niggers standing outside counting they money … that's a temptation.

Clearly there was a practical element involved: the public display of cash, fancy clothes and cars signaled that the individual in question had something of value to steal, yet offenders on the street often read a man's flossing as a direct masculinity challenge.

Snake's comments highlighted how flossing was read as a masculinity challenge by those who lacked the resources to floss themselves: 'We [Snake and his associates] were tired of seeing them [a group of drug dealers] just coming through, always trying to floss as they went past. We decided to tie 'em down 'cause we were trying to have a piece of the neighborhood crime.' Snake's discourse was layered. He indicated that the flossing was seen as a personal affront to him and his peers and that such resource displays made the men viable targets. By moving in on the neighborhood Snake felt was owned by him and his colleagues, the intruder's flashy display of wealth was a way to establish their reputation in the area. Victimizing the men enhanced the criminal capital Snake and his associates had in the neighborhood while simultaneously lowering that of their victims.

Moon described being victimized because of his own flossing: '[He] just was hating on me … I was making more money than him. I just told him I was making the usual thing. No, it was just some punk shit.' This discussion focused on the accumulation of masculine capital: Moon saw himself as superior because of his skills in the underground economy, whereas the violence directed at him was 'hating' and 'punk shit'. The juxtaposition of Snake's and Moon's comments metaphorically placed 'punkness' at each other's feet. Street masculinity, or at least informants' descriptions and definitions of such, was highly fluid and situational, with events recast for interviewers (and in the individual's own mind) in such a fashion as to highlight their own masculinity, while diminishing that of those around them.

Money

Conflicts over money and money producing (or losing) enterprises were commonly cited as reasons for violence between men. Street masculinity focuses on one's ability to obtain and conspicuously consume financial capital; when someone stole or cheated you out of these funds, your ability to enact masculinity was compromised. Any challenge to a man's 'business', a common referent for street crime among the sample, was a direct affront to his reputation and ability to continue in the fast-paced, money-intensive lifestyle of the streets.

CrazyJay described how he responded when a street associate took and extravagantly spent a large amount of his money:

> He blew like 400 of my dollars, probably close to $500. He stole my radio, my son's ring ... I wanted to fuck him up because I looked out for him. You bite the hand that feeds you, then that means that you need to be disciplined ... I didn't give a fuck who knew, I just wanted him to know, this is what you fucked up and if you ever, ever, ever decide to do that shit again, think about this first 'cause it gonna be even more severe, 'cause I could have stopped you from breathing ... I do got a conscience, I ain't just no motherfucking animal, man, but he took from me so I felt that was right ... he took from not only me, he took from my son.

CrazyJay justified the violence because the man had stolen from him, but the fact that he had stolen from CrazyJay's son intensified the perceived offense. He also drew on power hierarchies in his discussion, setting himself up as higher than the man who robbed him: now CrazyJay must 'discipline' him for his improper behavior. Discipline flows downwards in power hierarchies; Crazyjay saw himself as generally superior to the victim not only in terms of street status but also due to the fact that in the past he had 'looked out' for the man.

Jhustle discussed how he responded to a man stealing from him and then flaunting the stolen goods in front of him on the streets:

> His [the man who stole from Jhustle] cousin comes around bragging about how he got him some ... but I haven't seen the guy I gave the money to, but his cousin comes around like it don't matter. 'He took your motherfucking money.' That going to be it, you know what I'm saying, like I don't give a fuck about my money. Or my cell phone ... he's talking to himself in my face ... I'm like, man, you get out of my face, you know. He just kept on talking shit about me to getting my money and I just happened to have like a little crowbar in my hand ... he just kept pushing me and pushing me and pushing me. I wasn't gonna do nothing to him, and I just hit him across his face.

The inherent challenge was not just flossing, but rather it was flossing in front of a robbery victim with that victim's former property.

Black described how he responded when someone took marijuana from a stash box in his house, even though money was left as compensation:

> I had a box of blunts ... and I had left it there [at home] and when I came back my shit had been tampered with ... and when it came to me who did it ... they wasn't trying to mean to harm for real. Motherfucker left money. They was cool but that wasn't the point ... My shit wasn't for sale ... that was for me to smoke ... Motherfucker got beat down ... I got a pipe and I hit [him] upside his motherfucking head and split it there and put a big old pussy in his head.

The intent of the man was somewhat honest – money was left. As mentioned earlier in the chapter, Black and the man were longtime associates. Despite this, Black saw this as a violation of his personal space and masculinity, feeling the need to levy a rather severe sanction upon the man. Additionally, Black chose highly gendered language to describe the wound he inflicted. Putting a 'pussy in his head' is a phrase used to indicate the creation of a gaping wound in a victim that, to their eyes, looks like a woman's outer labia. This language was gendered in many respects. The comparison of the gaping wound to a vagina was clearly misogynistic; moreover, the term was used to feminize the victim.

Legitimate work

Although few of the men were frequently or steadily engaged in legitimate work, those who were discussed instances of perceived disrespect that provoked violence and retaliation in the workplace. The men who did work brought the values of the streets into the workplace, often resulting in their loss of the employment. TC, a barber, provided an elaborate discussion of vengeance he took on a co-worker who had wronged him by breaking his barber shears: '[H]e thought that I had done something to his stuff. See working in a shop is almost like a soap opera. There's a bunch of talking, you know what I'm saying. People lying on people.' Instead of responding immediately or violently, TC plotted out a sophisticated plot to attack the man's business well-being. TC began closely observing his routine, he 'timed him [the victim] to see what time he get to work, when he take his lunch break, when he step outside to smoke a cigarette' in order to find the most appropriate opportunity to exact revenge.

Ultimately he dropped the other man's clippers into a bowl of water: 'His shit rusted up ... when you cut the client it will nick them, that rust gets into their skin and it sets up an infection ... and they sue him ... for defective equipment.' Indeed, this is what happened.

> He nicked somebody ... at first he [the customer] ain't tripping off of it until it set up an infection. Then they say the big old thing, dude came back ready to whoop his ass, my homi [the co-worker] called the police, police come. So what happen he got sued, he wasn't licensed to practise here any more ... his licence got seized. You see one main thing is hygiene, health, cleanliness. State Board come in, like if this is a barber's shop, take about ten men, there was food around or if it was just not a clean environment, they would shut the place down.

Thus, instead of violence, TC attacked the man's livelihood – the same location of the offense against TC. However, as is more broadly understood on the streets, retaliation was called for and TC didn't care that someone else might get hurt in the process. Unlike many of the street-based episodes discussed earlier, the attack was neither immediate nor obvious. Yet the underpinning values of responding to attacks on one's masculinity, in this case TC's livelihood – a key way of doing masculinity for working-class men in the United States – were the same. Also, as described earlier in the chapter, TC was the individual who randomly attacked the supermarket patron to let off steam because his car had been vandalized.

Icy Mike, annoyed at the loss of his construction job, desired to respond on street terms: 'I was doing construction, but motherfuckers laid me off. I wish I could get his [his former supervisor's] ass and shit ... he's a bitch ass. He's cool but he's a punk.' Icy Mike interpreted his loss of gainful employment as a challenge to his autonomy and masculinity; he responded by placing his former boss into a subordinate masculinity. He continued, 'All I got to say [to the supervisor] is, "Fuck you." I want him to hear it.' Immediately after the above statement, the following exchange occurred in the transcript:

Interviewer: So retaliation's involved?
Icy Mike: Damn right, damn right. That's what it's for.

The latter statement implied at least a desire to respond with violence, even if it was not likely to happen. Overall, these excerpts highlight how embedded the ideals of street masculinity and its expected violence are among the men in the sample. Even in mainstream contexts, men actualizing street masculinity drew upon these codes of conduct, despite the fact that it would further isolate and alienate them from mainstream work and social networks.

The 'necessity' of violence

Many of the interviewees were asked why they felt the need to respond violently to masculinity challenges and other affronts. Particularly in the retaliation and snitch data sets, though less extensively in others, the data collectors probed the offenders about why they didn't rely on the police to settle disputes for them. Primarily, the offenders articulated the need to instill a raw form of vengeance upon those who wronged them, with no broader explanation than they saw it as necessary to respond with violence. Discussing how he and his peers responded to the murder of his brother, Duff coldly stated, 'My brother was killed in '92. OK, retaliation for that is the guy who killed him, we killed him.' Block also explained how he saw it in raw eye-for-an-eye terms: 'I rob a nigger dead and do whatever, just like he did to my people. He kill my people, I want him dead … If he whip my people we're going to whip him. If he shoot at my people, we gonna shoot at him … that's regardless if I was in the good life or the bad life.' Reflecting the broader cultural ideals of vengeance present in the Judeo-Christian epistemology, most of the men here discussed providing as much pain and suffering to their victimizers as they had suffered. Some, however, discussed coming back 'harder', using more violence in response than had been visited upon themselves. Not only was this often seen as a way to fully resolve the issue, it also placed the retaliator in a superior position in the hierarchy of the streets – instead of merely being 'even'.

Don Love's description of these norms emphasized the severity of the consequences if one doesn't retaliate against slights:

You can't let nobody beat you and your homies or whoever knows whose gotta beat you. It's like … it's always gonna be a issue of let this bullshit ride … Can't nobody hit you [with] something and then you just let it be … it's gotta be retaliation in the streets … You might let it be, you may not be tripping off of it but that guy see you or whatever … he might come up and rob you again or hit you across your damn head with a pistol

… just testing you … see where you heart is and if you don't do like shit about it, he gonna keep on picking at you or maybe he just might get rid of you.

Here the reputational, as well as practical, elements involved are highlighted. Don Love pointed out that failure to respond, and respond strongly, would set him up for potentially lethal victimization. Regardless of definitions of masculinity, such an articulated set of realities obviously produced serious and frequent violent reprisals in response to perceived and actual slights.

Many men felt the need to respond with violence to avoid appearing weak or being labeled a punk. Such discourse strongly linked this cyclical form of violence directly to masculinity and gender expectations. The following exchange between Lafonz and the interviewer highlighted the necessity of violence:

Interviewer: An eye-for-an-eye rule?
Lafonz: Yeah.
Interviewer: Why is that important out there?
Lafonz: It's real important out there … because if you let
                somebody hit you and you don't hit them back, then
                that's a sign of weakness. You're not holding your square
                … and if you're not holding you[r] square somebody's
                going to take it from you.

Similarly, Smokedog explained, 'If you let one motherfucker punk you, man, every motherfucker gonna try to punk you. I ain't going for that stuff cause no nigger's fucking with me.'

Jhustle echoed the same theme, but further cast it in terms of street hierarchies, drawing upon the metaphor of a parent–child relationship: "Cause if you don't do that [respond violently] then they'll [people on the streets] just run over you. Same way with kids. If you don't put your foot down with your kids they gonna run over you. Period. Sometimes you just got to put your foot down cause if you don't, motherfuckers gonna run over you.' Crazyjay also invoked the language of discipline in response to being stolen from: 'It's like a person is stealing my stuff, if they get away with it they gonna go back and try it again until they get caught … [but if I use violence against them] the next time they go up to steal they gonna think twice about the consequences … I think the disciplinary action gonna outweigh the other actions.' Such language re-emphasized the perceived power dynamics on the streets, with men always attempting to attain and maintain a superior position over others. The ability to legitimately use discipline derived from a man's superior position in a power hierarchy; discipline functioned as both retaliation and as exhibition of dominance.

The interviewers frequently asked questions concerning the interviewee's attitudes toward the police. Offenders expressed profoundly negative views of the police, seeing them as unreliable and corrupt, and considered calling them a sign of weakness (see also Rosenfeld, Jacobs and Wright 2003). These anti-police attitudes served to reinforce the push toward violent responses, as the police and law were not seen as viable modes of conflict resolution. Such attitudes were indeed political, a response to the intense alienation felt by African-Americans living in communities of concentrated poverty (see Anderson 1990, 1999). Many of the participants, however – especially those in the snitching and retaliation samples – directly tied this distrust of (and distaste for) the police to the previously discussed masculinity building elements of independence and self-reliance.

Beano's response was highly typical, not only in the rejection of the police but also in the explicit tie of that rejection to masculinity: 'Call in on somebody [to the police]? That's cowardly, like. I mean to me, like people on the street, soldiers that I know, that's just cowardly to do it that way. You a real man, stand on your own.' Similarly, Play Too Much said, 'Fuck the police, man. You can call them, they would never show up. They got their own stuff to worry about and that ain't gonna get nothing solved. I mean, why be labeled a snitch? That don't carry no weight on the street or in jail.' Here Play Too Much gave the three most frequently provided assessments of the police: (1) the police were uninterested in doing their job; (2) interacting with the police was snitching; and (3) if one was known on the streets for working with the police *in any way*, one's masculine capital was severely reduced, and that set him up for potential victimization.

Jack T expressed the broadly held disdain for the police on the streets and framed reliance upon the police as unmasculine. He felt he could, and should, deal with slights and injuries by himself:

Jack T: Why do I need the law when I can take care of myself? You know, this is myself.
Interviewer: What does that mean?
Jack T: I'm gonna see them if they rob me.
Interviewer: You'd retaliate?
Jack T: Oh, there ain't no doubt.

Big C expressed identical sentiments: 'I don't need the police to get in my business ... I don't need the police to take care of it ... if you can't handle your business yourself then you ain't got no business out there.'

In addition to the political, practical and gendered elements, some men saw imprisonment as insufficiently severe, and this motivated them to extract revenge themselves. When asked why he wouldn't allow the police to handle the resolution of a victimization, Sleezee-E identified the lack of perceived punishment that imprisonment represented:

> If you man enough or woman enough to say 'I had a row with somebody' and you think you can get away with it, then you get caught by the police and go to jail, you doing nothing but sitting on a tight spell, that's what you're doing while you're sitting in that jail, while we're out here sweating and stuff, working every day. You're sitting in there eating the food we're putting on your plate every day. There clothes on your back. So that ain't no justice.

Indeed, this echoed broader public sentiments often heard about prisons, but in this context the undercurrent is not a conservative annoyance at supporting criminals with tax dollars, but the understood assumption that if justice were visited on the offenders on the streets, it would be in the form of serious violence, not simply a loss of freedom.

These values and attitudes that demand violence to maintain one's reputation were deeply ingrained in the sample of offenders. The following exchange between the interviewer and Big Will highlighted how mainstream norms of civility and courtesy were replaced with deep expectations of violent response on the streets:

Interviewer: What if he would have said, 'Yeah it was me, I'm sorry'?

Big Will: Mm, that's a good one, that! 'Yeah it was me but I'm sorry.' I would have been sorry too but I would still have to get him! I'd have to beat him up and apologize too! 'Sorry for what I had to do but you had that coming!' This is payback.

Apologies and other face-saving dispute resolution techniques were thus seemingly absent from the repertoire of street men.

Conclusions

This chapter has focused on the exploration of how the demands of street masculinity generate and perpetuate street violence. Due to a lack of other capital, be it educational, financial or gendered, many men found themselves in possession of only one source of empowerment and prestige on the street: their reputation. This resource was constantly promoted and jealously guarded. The key way to earn and maintain reputation was to prove you were more violent and ruthless than your street associates.

Gender, especially the rigorous demands of street masculinity, framed and supported these violent approaches and self-presentations. Key elements of mainstream masculinity (e.g. self-sufficiency, toughness, independence) were refracted and magnified within this community of concentrated poverty, producing a set of behavioral expectations for men that demanded they establish their manhood through violence. Unlike other locales within American social structure, the use of violence to establish dominance in peer group hierarchies did not fade with the passing of adolescence; without educational and occupational resources to draw upon in the construction of an adult masculinity, most of the men in this study relied on interpersonal violence as a key tool in building and maintaining their 'name' within streetlife networks.

With one's reputation constantly at stake, and any hold on pre-eminence or prestige never more than tenuous, even the most minor disrespect or insult seemed to provoke harsh reprisals from the most deeply embedded interviewees. Although the offenders provided explanations for this violence that were strongly practical in nature (e.g. victimization avoidance), the language they used was clearly gendered. Being a man and being a respected, powerful person on the streets were one and the same. Failures within street hierarchies were failures of masculinity; successful violent retaliation enhanced one's manhood.

In the next chapter I will explore how street masculinity shaped interactions between men and women in these communities. The powerful misogyny that guided men's interactions with other men also shaped their interactions with the women in their lives.

Notes

1 Peon is not a street term specifically. It generally indicates someone of low status, at the bottom of the hierarchy. It derives from the Mexican peonage system of agricultural stratification, referring to peasant farmers. In USA usage, it gained coinage from its unintentional punning on 'pee (urinate) on'.

2 'Freak', 'Rat', 'Hood rat' and 'Wreck' are all words used on the streets to refer to a promiscuous woman.

Chapter 5

One man's 'ho' is another man's sister: men's relationships with women and families

So far, women have been noticeably absent from the bulk of my discussions of life in streetlife social networks. We have seen how women can serve as masculine capital (see Chapter 3) and how they can provoke masculinity challenges between street combatants (see Chapter 4). Indeed, especially from the perspective of men, women played a highly peripheral role on the streets; social networks were heavily gender-segregated. However, to fully understand masculinity as an aspect of social structure and as a set of enacted behaviors, it is fruitful to explore inter-gender relationships as well. A given masculinity is defined in reference not only to other masculinities, but also to existing femininities. Masculinities strongly dictate how interactions between the genders should occur, and frame the different categories into which women are placed by men. This chapter begins by analyzing men's existing perceptions of women within the social context of streetlife; it will then explores how these gender categories interact with masculinities by looking at the various ways in which men interact with women in their daily lives.

In this area the data are honestly thinnest. Whereas every interviewee was asked about marital status and the number of children they had, typically these queries were asked at the end of the interview for demographic purposes (in the context of also asking about age, education, etc.) and were not probed. Thus the offenders often had to interject discussions of these elements of their own accord (consciously or unconsciously). As the interviews focused on the nature and dynamics of specific criminal offenses, topics of interest here were often not forefronted. Yet there is enough discussion of inter-gender dynamics in the data to explore relationships. Further, due to the dialectical and oppositional nature of gender definitions, it is crucial to understand inter-gender social network interactions to fully understand the nature of masculinities on the streets of Saint Louis and how these gender constructs interact and intersect with violent criminality.

Overall, I discovered three available cognitive categories into which men place women on the streets: (1) 'whores' to be exploited; (2) wives and girlfriends; and (3) female blood relatives (e.g. grandmothers, mothers, sisters and cousins). Overall, women in the first category were seen by the men here as weak, untrustworthy and not worth bothering with in a personally invested manner. However, these attitudes toward women, and the rules for interacting with them, are complex and contradictory. The role demands of street masculinity situated kin as meriting significantly different treatment than non-kin. While unrelated women were typically discussed as vehicles for the fulfillment of men's criminal objectives and sexual desires, female relatives were objects of protection. This chapter first explores men's attitudes and their described interactions with women on the streets, then looks at how men's domestic-centered relationships with family members (wives, mothers, sisters and children) influence and spill over (or fail to) into their streetlife behaviors, especially violence.

Men and women on the streets

Negative attitudes toward women

Most qualitative work on women in street-corner social contexts has emphasized the marginal positions women hold and the intense sexism they face on a daily basis (see Bourgois 1995, 1996; Maher 1997; Miller 2001; Mullins 2006; Steffensmeier 1983; Steffensmeier and Terry 1986). Such attitudes were not absent from men interviewed here. Due to the nature of the interviews, most of these accounts arose when men discussed violent or potentially violent encounters that evolved over women (see Chapter 4).

When asked about a potentially violent encounter with a man over a woman, Play Too Much expressed disdain for women in general: '[It] shouldn't have went that far [to get violent] ... over something temporary.' In his mind, the tenuous and fragile nature of inter-gender relationships made them not worthy of the risks associated with interpersonal violence on the streets. For Play Too Much, and many of the men here, any sort of social tie to a woman was brief and focused on desire satisfaction. Later, when asked about using sex to get back at a woman who had wronged him, the same interviewee made similarly dismissive statements: 'Women ain't acting like that, I'll go get another one. Don't chase them, just replace them.' This, again, emphasizes the temporary nature of sexual-romantic bonds. As we saw in Chapter 3, the high value men placed on independence and freedom produced (and reinforced) fragile connections with their female peers.

T Dog summed up his view of women's worth by saying, 'It just a woman.' This dominant attitude was clear and common among interviewees: women were replaceable, disposable objects to be given no respect of consequence.[1] Speezy's attitude toward women was clear in his statement: 'I don't even mess with women, my friend had her, he had her, I had her, I just drop her and do what I gotta do.' Snap jokingly responded to a question about whether he would target a woman in a drug robbery: 'I wouldn't rob a woman ... I be too busy trying to get in they pants, you see what I'm saying.' These excerpts illustrated the categorization of women as objects valuable immediately prior to and during a sexual conquest, but only valuable later in so far as the man's brief possession of her added to his overall sexual and masculine reputation. Men also frequently verbalized rape myths and other similarly misogynistic attitudes when describing the sexuality of the women they interacted with. TC explained: 'Women love sex twice as much as we love it, matter of fact, even more. And all you got to do is basically do what they do. See, they do it silently, women they wear clothes and stuff enough to show their body proportion.'

Female co-offenders

Long-standing co-offending relationships between men and women were rarely mentioned in the data. In the few examples uncovered, the women clearly held marginal positions. Women were occasionally mentioned as drivers or simply acknowledged as being present with no discussion of their precise role. None of the men described long-term relationships of this nature; the examples of these relationships came from women in the sample. A few of the women mentioned selling drugs as part of a male-dominated social network; when they did discuss such activities, they often acknowledged their marginalized status. For example, Stacy explained, '[I did] a little bit

of dealing with cannabis for money but I was way down the chain
– I didn't help make it or nothing like that.' Ladybug was very clear
about who was in charge in a long-term, co-offending relationship.
'I been doing it [offending with the same man] for ten years, eleven
years basically we been together. I do what he tells me to do 'cause
he cover my back.' Apart from these examples, three clearly defined
roles for women in male-dominated offending groups emerged from
both male and female interviews: (1) women served as key sources of
information for men; (2) men used women to carry contraband (e.g.
guns and drugs) to avoid potential criminal charges; and (3) men
used women to set up other men for violent victimization.

Men in the sample discussed drawing upon women as sources of
information on the streets. Since many men frequently undervalued
and overlooked women in their interactions and networks, they often
did not take care to conceal information from them. Further, they
also tended not to know who the women knew or talked to. Other
men knew this and used women when trying to find out who had
victimized them in a robbery or when trying to locate an individual
they had targeted for retaliatory violence. Often, men framed this
information gathering as simply overhearing conversations or from
women volunteering the information to them. Looney Ass Nigger
described how he and his friends found out where some people who
had recently robbed them were hanging out: 'Well, some girls came
and told [us that a] couple of them, these cats are ... making static ...
She [one of the girls] say "Hey, they down at the dope house."' The
interviewee and his peers went down to the crack house, then robbed
and beat the men. Block described how he learned the identity and
location of a man who had robbed him: "Cause he told his gal and
his gal cool with my gal ... not that he knew they was cool ... They
just know each other ... and they just gossiping.' When necessary,
men went to the often present but typically overlooked women in
streetlife contexts to glean information needed.

Research suggests that Saint Louis police do not pay as much
attention to women as potential offenders when identifying would-be
street criminals (see Jacobs 1999, 2000; Jacobs and Miller 1998; Miller
2001). Male and female interviewees claimed that women were less
frequently searched for weapons or drugs and that the searches that
were done tended to be less thorough, and scrutiny less intense. Men
acted upon this knowledge and used women to carry contraband for
them to lessen the chances they would incur legal penalties. Often
this was at the expense of the women with whom they interacted.
Goldie explained:

> I know my little freaks are bickered [carrying a weapon] up all
> the time. If I'm gonna get with them, then I know they got a
> weapon, 'cause the cops will sweat a nigger before they sweat
> a bitch ... If ... I'm with a new little honey or a new freak or
> something that I met, and she don't know how I get down or
> I'm just taking her out, then I'm bickered up 'cause I don't know
> about her for real ... I don't want to get her into no trouble.

Despite the implication of a chivalrous attitude toward women in
not asking 'new' girls to carry contraband for him, Goldie and other
men in the sample had no problems exploiting women for their own
benefit. Goldie's description also showed that the main reason is not
the protection of the girl; since he wouldn't 'know about her for real'
he would place himself at risk. This risk would not only be in the
form of the girl potentially snitching to the police about Goldie's
activities, but also if he was not sure of her character and loyalties
and a situation arose in which he needed a firearm, he couldn't be
sure how the girl would react. It would have done him little good to
have her carrying a weapon if she was likely to run away or break
down in hysterics if the use of the weapon was called for.

Such practices were confirmed by the women interviewed. Frizz
explained how she frequently hid drugs and weapons on her person
at the bequest of men she interacted with: '[You] stick it down in your
bra. They're [the police] not gonna be searching you and pulling your
bra all up and I'm not gonna be seen, I'm not gonna give them any
reason to stop me. I'm gonna be dressed nice, prettiest of figures.' By
playing to perceived stereotypes, Frizz's ability to carry contraband
for herself or a male associate was distinctly enhanced. Smooth G
also described similar behaviors and rationales: 'They [the police]
ain't gonna mess with me 'cause usually how I dress, you wouldn't
even imagine. What her? Like she dressed? Strapped?' Both women
described specific perceptions the police had not only in regard to the
general dangerousness of females but to the belief that if a woman
appeared to be fulfilling a more emphasized femininity – displayed
through typical, more conservative dress – then the amount of risk
she presented was low indeed. To further emphasize her point on the
folly of such thought, immediately after the above quoted excerpt,
Smooth G indicated that she was currently carrying a gun in her
purse, showing it to the interviewers.

One of the most frequent ways men drew upon women to assist
them in offending was by using a female's appearance of sexual
availability to set men up to be victimized. This behavior played

off men's blind-spots in relation to the potential danger posed by women (one does not fear the object of exploitation). It also entailed a significant amount of risk to the woman involved. J-Rock explained how he set a guy up with the help of a woman: 'He [the victim] got a girlfriend and I was fucking this gal, you know, back then. I said, "The man up there" – she keeps him in bed sleeping – "you let me in there", so I told her, "I'm gonna get this nigger." No clothes, running down the street and I got him.'

Some of the men's discussions highlighted coercion in the use of women as decoys. Bacca described using a woman who was not a willing participant in order to accomplish a victimization:

> Well it's this girl, well we're riding with him [the intended victim] right, and it's this girl we knew so we pull up on the side of her and he's talking to her. You know, he liked her, he just wanted to have sex with her … So we're thinking, when we get home we're thinking, like damn, how can we make some money? So I say, 'He liked the girl, so we gonna ask her about it and if it's ok with her, she want to go through with it, we can do it, we can cut her off something too' … We just came straight out and asked her, was she down for it? … She said no but we just bugged her, we told her she had to do it … we just tried to scare her so she can go through with it. So she finally went through with it, but she didn't take anything at the end.

While the woman used as a decoy did have sex with the victim, it was only after cajolement and coercion. Then, after acquiescing to the demands of Bacca and his friends, she was still cut out of the proceeds of the crime. When men discussed using this tactic, the potential danger to the woman was never mentioned. For those who employed this tactic, once the robbery or retaliation was accomplished, the decoys were discarded like one would get rid of a gun with a body on it. The crime done, the tool was of no use until it was needed again.

Several instances of men being victimized by this tactic were also recorded. Goldie's description of being caught unaware in this fashion was typical:

> So me and my little girl we were just standing there talking and we heard them, 'Get up!' You know, there were four guys. One had a gun, one was taking off my stuff, one was taking off her stuff and one was the look-out … after they done all of that,

you know, I thought it was a set-up because once the baby girl got on the bus or whatever and went on home, she called me saying they'd returned her stuff.

It was only after the last revelation about the girl's 'stuff' being returned that Goldie finally realized he was set up. K-Red also described a similar victimization:

I had me a little gal down there ... She tried to [get] me jumped. She tried to get me set up ... She had called my house, told me to go down to her house. I was scared to go down there anyway ... She told me to come down there ... I come down there, after that, I go down there. She's up there like ... and this dude [a drug dealer whom K-Red had robbed previously] had came up the elevator and I had to run down the fire escape.

K-Red narrowly escaped the dealer's retaliation.

Every women in the sample described several cases in which they had, at the bequest of men, presented themselves as sexually available to targets of their male peers' violent depredations. Primarily, this provided an element of surprise to the victimization. YoYo provide a typical description of how such a set-up would be played out:

Well, men carried the gun ... 'cause they got a lot of dope, crack, and they want some sex so they want to exchange sex for dope. At the same time you in there you talking to him and he getting undressed ... you know the signal. You holler out a name or say a certain word ... then that [is] when they [male co-offenders] come in and that's when you get him. He already out of his clothes, so what can he do? He can't do nothing. [We then take the] guns and dope and run like hell, he can't do nothing but stand there buck naked and get beat down and here we go.

Smooth G's description concurred with YoYo's, but she went so far as to identify this as the best and preferred method of victimizing men, especially drug dealers:

The best way a dope man can get set up is by a female 'cause [he] gonna look at her like yeah, I can hit her [have sex with her], I can hold this. But ... that's where [he is] wrong ... you just in the bathroom stripping, taking your clothes off to get in the shower ... they [male co-offenders] just came through the door on you and if they took me out with a gun to my head, you would not think that I tried to set this up, especially if they slap me around, that's just all part of the game.

Smooth G noted that to make the set-up more convincing, the woman's role needed to be framed as a victim as well, thereby avoiding suspicion that what happened was indeed a set-up. Big Mix also emphasized this aspect of the set-up in her description:

I acted like I was going to take him home, lay him real good ... that gets them every time ... When they [her male co-offenders] jacked him or whatever, he just ran. And I screamed like I act like I didn't know what was going on and I ran ... like I'm a victim too, like I don't know what's going on, you know. I mean, I was just screaming and hollering.

It is clear from the women in the sample that even though their actions were central to carrying out the offense, their position within the group and within the reward structure of the group was marginal. Several women mentioned being struck by the men during the charade to obfuscate her role in the scheme. Additionally, none of the interviewees mentioned the rewards women might have gained from these endeavors.

Broadly, this phenomenon is well known in the qualitative literature on street crime, especially within studies of female offending (see Katz 1988; Maher 1997; Miller 1998; Mullins and Wright 2003). In the current study, it was the primary fashion in which women seeking to victimize men could take advantage of a key male blind spot: an inattention to women's ability to victimize them. However, throughout the data, almost all of these set-ups were orchestrated by men, and men were the primary beneficiaries of this tactic. So, while in some cases women used this approach to negotiate male-dominated street culture and offending networks, it was also another way in which men dominated and exploited their female peers.

A final type of exploitation of women by men on the streets revolved around street-level sex work. While neither deeply discussed nor probed by the interviewers, pimp–prostitute relations emerged on a few occasions within the context of a violent encounter the men had gotten into over the prostitute in question. DL explained how he was assaulted by another man 'about a woman. She was making money for me and she wanted to change everything.' While it was unclear if the women DL spoke of wanted out of prostitution or just wanted to change pimps, the confrontation between the men turned violent: the man eventually stabbed DL because he would not let the woman go. A few events such as this were raised in the data, some of which were clearly cases of a woman trying to escape prostitution by leaving her pimp for the protection of another man. The interviewees derisively referred to this as 'trying to turn a whore into a housewife'. The focus of the derision was typically not the marginalized women, but the man who sought to invest social and personal capital into such a woman.

Play Too Much discussed an incident of violence that emerged when he had his cousin protect one of his women. While this is the putative job of a pimp, this was the only example of this sort of behavior recorded in the data: 'One of my girls was with a guy [a customer], basically a guy who was hurting her, so the word was on the street and he [Play Too Much's cousin] got into it with this guy [the customer].' While Play Too Much did not carry out the violence himself, his cousin was acting in Play Too Much's interests. Icy Mike described a situation (discussed in the previous chapter) in which a man picked up one of his women in a club. According to Icy Mike, the action resulted in violence, not because the man picked up his woman, but because of the attitude the man displayed:

> We was at the club. Motherfucker was trying to haul out with one of my little bitches. I don't give a fuck about the bitch 'cause I got somebody at home [a live-in girlfriend], it don't even matter, but the thing is this old boy is trying to holler at the bitch and then he want to throw it in my face. Like 'I'm on this bitch, what you gonna do about it?' ... 'I don't give a fuck about her, you can fuck her.' But he's getting too high with this shit ... too confident ... so I got to let him know. 'You tripping, you showing your ass up to this motherfucking doll' ... I tried to keep it all peaceful and shit but he want to take it all the wrong way ... my niggers got on him, my people got on top of him.

As discussed earlier, this incident again highlights the disdain Icy Mike felt toward the women in his life.

Overall, when interacting with women in streetlife social contexts, men's treatment of them was guided by strongly misogynistic values. The data shows little indication of beliefs concerning equality or respect. Men seemed to approach women in these social situations first and foremost as vehicles for the fulfillment of their immediate desires and objectives. This was clearly indicative of the sexism which permeated the streets. Yet, men held strikingly different attitudes when interacting with their families, especially their female blood relatives.

Men and families

The juvenile delinquency literature is rich in explorations of the influence (or lack thereof) of an individual's family and delinquency. Especially for boys, such factors as the number of parents in the household, the strength of the relationships between parents and children, the amount of surveillance a child receives and the delinquency of both parents and siblings have been well investigated and documented. However, the relationship between adult offending and family relationships is less well established. Sampson and Laub's (1993) reanalysis of the Gleuck data suggests that a strong marriage serves as a key transition out of offending. Other work has also documented the relationship between having a normative spouse or significant other and an overall trend toward criminal desistance (see Giordano, Cernkovich and Rudolf 2002; Mullins and Wright 2003). Thus, criminology provides a general picture of family bonds – for both adults and children – as having a negative influence on criminal behavior. However, it is also conceivable that the same relationship could have an opposite effect.

In his exploration of life in Germantown, Anderson (1990, 1999) suggests that violence can be produced by a strong bond to a family member. Specifically, in a neighborhood dominated by the code of the streets, men and boys may be called upon to wield violence to protect their family from predators.

Although data collection was not expressly designed to elicit information about the lives and social relationships of men and women beyond their offending behavior, their descriptions of events and people nonetheless shed some light on the nature and structure of the offenders' social networks. Never directly asked about their families and romantic relationships (save demographic questions about marital status and number of children), men wove discussions about these aspects of their lives into their discussions of violence, especially retaliatory violence. Here I explore to the extent possible the nature and dynamics of these relationships and how they were intertwined with street violence.

Wives and romantic partners

Of the 86 men in the sample, only nine (10.5 per cent) reported being married at the time of the interview (in four cases there was no mention of marital status in the interview). This, combined with the lack of questions concerning marital interactions, makes it not unsurprising that few mentioned spouses in their interviews. In fact, apart from the yes/no question 'Are you married?' only two men made mention of their wives within the interviews. The following discussion was prompted by the interviewer asking the offender how he balanced his relationship with his wife and the numerous relationships he had with other women in the neighborhood. Goldie responded:

> That's just me. It ain't like I'm getting back at my wife [by having sex with other women], I'm just being me. I like women and this [girl in question] is just a whore ... I go to hotels [to have affairs] ... [My wife] is just a house lady. She don't go out. She don't mess with me. She stay home with the kids ... [She's a] good wife.

Goldie's description highlighted the strongly segregated nature of streetlife in Saint Louis. Though he was involved in a mainstream relationship, he strongly separated the criminal aspects of his life from domestic relationships. If this is a pattern that holds across the other married men in the sample, it explains why their wives were never mentioned (the second mention, quoted later, merely indicated her existence).

Romantic partners were mentioned with a slightly greater frequency than wives, but in no way constituted a significant portion of the data. When they were discussed, it was with highly negative connotations and little elaboration as to the nature of the relationship or its more mundane aspects. Kilo, for example, framed his relationships as another way he 'got over' on the streets:

> I got a lot of girlfriends, they got money ... most of them well off. You can get $200 or $300 at the first of the month and then go cop, get some dope ... you act like you like 'em, you know, you might really like them. But let me get $200. Do this and that and the other, whatever you tell them, whatever you got to tell them.

Elsewhere in the interview, Kilo mentioned maintaining a relationship with a woman in the suburbs solely for the purpose of having a safe house to hide out in when he needed to escape potential violence in his neighborhood. Don Love only mentioned his current relationship in the context of explaining why he had violently victimized someone: 'I was kind of mad [which is why I beat the guy up], which I should have just chilled because I had a little beef with my [girlfriend] or whatever. She was talking about threatening to throw me out of the crib or whatever so I was, like, kind of being ... hard headed ... so I'm like, man, fuck it. I'm on my own.' Commitment to a long-term relationship, or at least presenting oneself as being within such a relationship, violated key tenets of street masculinity regarding independence and self-sufficiency, discussed in Chapter 3. While many masculinities in western society at least playfully denigrate romantic commitment, here it appeared to be much more serious: here the men's lives, to a greater extent, seemed to match their rhetoric.

The women in the sample were just as disparaging of romantic ties as the men. When asked if she was married, Ladybug responded:

Don't nobody want to marry me 'cause they say I'm too mean. I act like a man. This one dude I'm dating now, I had to beat his ass. He's scared of me. He said don't bring no gun into my house 'cause I told him my stories and stuff. But when that bitch want some [of] the money, he know how to call and then there go my dumb ass. All right, let me go hit a set or something [commit an armed robbery].

Despite her apparent dissatisfaction with the man and her relationship with him, and her independent presentation of self, Ladybug found herself acquiescing to his demands for cash by committing crimes to satisfy his requests.

Nicole offered a similar description of her romantic prospects: 'I ain't got no man in my life. I'm too thuggish for that ... we would be ready to kill each other then. Ain't no lie. He can't like what I like to do and he trying to do it and trying to keep me at home, no.' Similarly, Popo described her latest relationship: 'Well I did [have a man in my life] ... but he don't fuck with me either. I'm saying he want to be with me when I want to go out and do some dirt. I can come out with some money or some dope, he cool. Shit, fuck him. [He only came around] when he want pussy or something.' Seemingly, the women embedded in streetlife networks responded to the exploitation and disdain of men by dismissing their overall importance. While the men tended to dismiss women because of their own intense sexist attitudes, the women were equally dismissive of the men as a result of repeated disrespectful experiences at men's hands. This could well be a function of their experiences with such men in the past and a general movement toward the adoption of masculine attitudes in some areas due to long-term exposure to streetlife.

When present in specific social interaction, romantic partners did appear to have a slight moderating effect on whether a social encounter turned violent. A minor sub-theme concerning the effects of women on violence emerged during data analysis. While the interviews focused on violent crimes committed, occasionally they recorded incidents of halted actions.[2] Among the descriptions of aborted violence, the presence of a woman in the interaction was frequently cited as the reason. Consequently, women's presence could moderate potential violence, if only delaying it until another time.

D-Boy described an incident in which he was threatened but not victimized: 'He's [the offender threatening D-Boy] like, "I could get you right now." But, see, I was with my girl, you know, and that's a witness. Which they don't give a fuck these days and he seen she was pregnant. So he was like, "Yeah, man, it's all good, but ain't never forgotten" … he was up on me. He had me.' D-Boy's implication was that if the man in question had victimized him, he would have had to victimize the woman he was with, also ('that's a witness'); her pregnancy was identified as the reason that the violent encounter was diffused. Norms of masculine protection of women and particularly the negative light in which violence against a pregnant woman was framed, seem to have guided the potential assailant.

The following exchange between Big Will and an interviewer also exhibits this potentially moderating effect of women:

Interviewer: What would they [a potential victim] have to say to talk their way out if it?

Big Will: I do not know. It depends on how it's done, on whether I'm with a lady friend of mine or not.

Here, the presence of a romantically involved woman with a potential offender restricted his violence.[3] Bacca made reference to family ties in explaining why he avoided a specific violent retaliation: 'I didn't go through with it [a retaliation] … I mean, his sister, well, that's my daughter's mother. Well, [he is] my daughter's uncle. I didn't go through with it 'cause I had a baby by his sister.' However, as the data here focused more on criminal events carried out rather than criminal events aborted, the precise nature and extent of this moderating influence remains unclear.

Mothers, sisters and cousins

While men's discussions of women in a street context emphasized sexist attitudes and exploitive behavior, their discussions of female blood relatives revealed attitudes that were significantly more respectful. The men typically discussed using violence to protect or exact revenge for their female family members. As discussed earlier, protection of perceived social subordinates was a key element of street masculinity (and normative masculinity). Red's remarks were typical: 'It's all about if you hurt somebody that I love, then I'm gonna hurt somebody you love. If you make my mama cry, then I'm gonna make your mama cry and this gonna go all back and forth.'

In the context of discussing various criminal events, a few men mentioned their mothers. In most contexts, attitudes and influences of mothers were strongly different from those of the women men viewed as their peers or inferiors. Black made the strongest, and simplest, statement of this sentiment within the sample: 'Man, I got one motherfucking friend … my mama is my only motherfucking friend.'

Some of the men who interjected discussions of their mothers discussed specifically how their mothers were crucial in curtailing their violent behavior. TC described why he let a victimization against him slide: '[My brother] he got that [execution by lethal injection][4] in 1972, so you know, to show my mama how much I love her, so I wouldn't end up like him, I didn't retaliate. I just let it go.' Red, one of the most violent men in the data set, explained how his mother talked him out of a retaliation. Red and his brother had gotten into a fight with two other men. The other men were using baseball bats as weapons and Red was seriously injured. He went home, planning to retaliate against them, but:

> My mama really told me to leave it, but I didn't want to let it go … I still trip off that today [some years after the event] … that's the only thing she ever talked me out of really … She was like, 'It's not worth it. Don't look for him. You know you got your kid out here, you know, you trying to raise your kid.[5] Don't let him send you to the penitentiary … I know he done

mess[ed] your mouth up, your mouth busted [and] all, and I know it hurt, but just do it for me.' I'm like, 'Yeah, mama.'

Other men mentioned the victimization of their mother – whether slight or severe – as a catalyst for retaliatory violence. Discussing a violent encounter, Chewy said, 'I'll probably get him [beat him up] again because he cursed in front of my mama.' Smokedog described a retaliation he carried out on his mother's behalf:

He [the victim] use to be [a] dope fiend … use to try and cheat dope fiends. Well he [physically] hit my mama and choked up [smoked] like $20 or some shit [in drugs]. Later we say 'We got [to] get that bubby.' … He [physically] hit my mama … [I found the man on the streets, and confronted him. He said] 'Damn, what you doing, dude?' [I said] 'You hit my mama. That what I'm doing.' He tried to run and [I] hit him in the ass. Boom! Boom, boom, boom, boom [shooting] … He ran. He got around the corner and jumped in his car and drove off.

Smokedog claimed never to have encountered the man again.

Whereas mothers occupied a distinct social space, separate from the more typical views about women on the streets, sisters and other female relatives were also defined differently from street corner associates. Men mentioned specific incidents in which they violently victimized other men to rectify slights and victimizations against their female kin. Player discussed at length his assaults of a man who had severely and repeatedly beaten up his sister. Even though he claimed to have already beaten the man up, and the man was in prison for the prior assaults, Player still saw the need for more violence:

Motherfucker blind[ed] my sister's eye. Broke her fucking nose and just fucked her up … They can't give him enough time. I'm still gonna fuck him up whenever I see him. He's asking for that, man. That's respect. There's no motherfucking way my sister could whoop him, big ol' motherfucker like that. Oh yeah, I'm gonna put a pussy in his head whenever I see him and I'm not going to go up and try to punch this motherfucker, understand. I'm gonna put a pipe on his motherfucking ass and when I get him to where I know I got him, I'm gonna lay hands on him.

Player emphasized the unfairness behind the man's violence, as his sister was unable to respond in kind ('there's no way my sister could whoop him'); as discussed in Chapter 3, this attack on a female was typically seen on the streets as unmasculine or punk behavior. Additionally, Player had a gender-defined duty to protect his sister and respond to the man's violence.

Bishop discussed a long-running conflict he had with a man who had frequently beaten Bishop's sister while she was pregnant:

> My sister was seeing this gentleman … [He] knew about me and my friends and yet he still insisted on seeing my sister after we warned him … I found out that he had got my sister pregnant and then refused to take responsibility for it … and then on top of that, he beat her … First we threatened him to try to get him to take responsibility, but it didn't work … talked to him, tell him, first I was nice to him because he did have some ties in the neighborhood … I wanted to keep some peace. When that didn't work I got into several confrontations with him and it was getting worse each time … [I tried to tell him to] stop touching her, stop hitting her … and it started getting worse … A few times he walked away with a broken nose. I think we [Bishop and his friends] broke his hip one time … [When I was beating him I] said stuff like 'You're no good if you can't take responsibility for your actions, so you're going to take responsibility for what you did. Until [you] show [your] face and come clean I'm [gonna] keep doing this to you.' … I always consider if you attack my family, you attack me and if you ask anyone else, especially anyone that grew up in my neighborhood, that's pretty much how the mentality is. You attack the family of somebody, you attack them personally.

The demands of masculinity to protect one's kin are at the core of Bishop's ongoing violence. Unlike other respondents, Bishop exhibited a reference to and connection with more mainstream masculinities in that he emphasized that he originally sought a non-violent solution to the problem. Additionally, the man in question deserved Bishop's violence for two key failures of masculinity: (1) not taking responsibility for his sexual behaviors; and (2) being violent with a romantic partner. While the former was generally seen as a broad tenet of street masculinity, Bishop's narrative highlighted the strong contrast in the acceptability of this behavior when the woman in question was 'just a woman' as opposed to when she was a family member. In other places, Bishop shifted back and forth between which bothered him more, with the former reason often outweighing the latter. He emphasized his sister's pregnancy as the key reason the violence was improper and unmanly. Later in his description of the incidents he justified his anger and violence toward the man repeatedly beating his sister and hitting her in the abdomen by claiming, 'He was trying to take the baby!'[6]

Female offenders confirmed these patterns as they also frequently discussed seeking the assistance of men in their social networks, both street and family, to resolve insults and potentially violent encounters. Further, when such incidents were mentioned, the interviewees almost always connected this assistance to gender. Miss Dee simply explained, 'by me being a female, people kind of look out for me'. Lady Ice described how she responded to a male's victimization of her at a bar: 'We were at a club and one of the guys smacked me and I went out and I got [my male relatives] and they came over and they beat the guy up ... pretty bad ... I can't beat up [a guy] I mean, I could try but I don't think I would win.' Pooh Bear also discussed drawing on her male peers to exact vengeance on a man who had wronged her by not paying her money she felt was due:

> This guy I met at a club, you know we danced the night right into the morning ... He told me that he would hook me up [pay her money], you know, 'cause I slept with him. So he didn't do that ... I asked him for $1,000. So I slept with him the same night ... then I didn't see him ... Two weeks later I see him at the club again. I said, 'Hey I got something for you.' Told my [male] partners to hook him up. He tricked me ... and that's what he got, his ass whooped ... He tried to go get his friends but they started fighting again so the police came over ... His friend got shot on the lot ... You see, he played me. So that's what he got, he got his ass whooped and his partner got shot. You don't play with nobody like that ... I had my [male] friend do it ... 'cause I'm too little and he's a big guy.

All the women distinctly linked their utilization of men to provide violent 'back-up' as a function of their gender.[7] One key difference between men's and women's discussion of these events is that men never mentioned using violence as a means of protecting their street peers (with the exception of pimps and their prostitutes).[8] Rather, men's narratives focused on avenging family members. Women, on the other hand, talked more frequently about seeking assistance from street peers and only rarely talked about getting help from their families.

Children and fatherhood

Of the men interviewed, nearly two-thirds (64 per cent) claimed to have at least one child.[9] Despite the high prevalence of fatherhood among the interviewees, only about one third mentioned them in the interviews outside of the question that asked how many children they had.[10] Those who did discuss their children identified the need to provide for them as a motivation for violent offending. Bacca, discussing his cousin's offending, explained, 'He have kids, he don't have money and this and this and that … he needed money [for the kids].' Low, who worked full time, explained that he still needed to engage in street crime: 'I have to support my family with the checks I get from the temp service … like I'm getting paid … $5.65 [an hour].' To fully provide for his family and also maintain his involvement in a party-centered lifestyle, Low resorted to robbery. Similarly, Blackwell explained how he used the proceeds from his robberies: 'I buy clothes, I pay bills, I give my son money … I give my daughter money, I buy groceries for the house.' Raydog explained the motivation for a robbery as an answer to the same social demands of fatherhood, 'I was down there with my son and my son kept pressing me for some new Nikes and I didn't have the money, so I had to do it [a robbery] for my baby.' Kow offered the same rationale for a robbery: '[to] buy my baby a pair of tennis shoes.'

Low explained two driving forces behind his crimes: 'I be messing with heroin … and my daughter needed shoes and shit like that and my girlfriend was pressuring me about getting her some shoes … baby food and stuff like that … get her shoes, some more clothes, [plus] something to take care of my habit.' Likewise, C-Low discussed how an associate of his was 'driven' to street crime by his parental status:

He was doing, like, his business, 'cause he has to do shit to take care of his daughter and shit, and his baby. And his baby's mother was doing so much shit [drugs], he felt it was time he had to do something, do it for his baby, but she [his baby's mother] look at him like it's wrong, but he gotta … do [what he's got to do] to take care of his family, and shit like that. I

respect that, you know? You got to rob to take care of your kid.
I respect that. You gotta take care of yours.

Here, offending was framed within the context of actualizing
masculinity as a provider for one's family, even when other
motivations or uses of the money coincided. Fulfilling the demands
of fatherhood was cited as a reason to engage in criminality; the
masculinized nature of this was further highlighted by the respect
and esteem which C-Low gave to his friend for enacting the role.[11]
He emphasized, 'You gotta take care of yours.' This was especially
salient because the children's mother was deeply involved in drug
use. As with other aspects of street masculinity, this was a clear
example of the sort of refraction of more generally held masculinity
demands (e.g. being an economic provider for one's children and
gaining esteem for it from others) within street masculinity.

On the other hand, a few men discussed the presence, or impending
presence, of children as a factor pushing them toward criminal
desistance rather than offending. As Bishop explained:

I got a daughter of my own I need to watch out for now, and
the worst thing is if he [someone Bishop was in a retaliation
cycle with] does come back and I can't get to him, or he does
get my sister or my daughter, that would be retaliation and once
you really start it, you're kind of stuck, because you retaliate on
somebody and they're going to come back ... It's just gonna
keep going round in circles and I really don't want that for my
daughter.

D-Boy echoed Bishop's sentiments: 'Hopefully it [a current retaliation
cycle] don't escalate into nothing else ... 'cause I got a baby due. The
due date is tomorrow ... this is my first child.' Similarly, J explained,
'I got married, got a wife, trying to raise my son, trying to do things
right, you know, 'cause it weren't leading nowhere, 'cause I weren't
getting nowhere.' Three-Eye was non-committal about whether his
status as a father would lead to desistance, but was clearly feeling
some pressure in that direction: 'I'll never stop, though I'm planning
on getting away from all that, you know. I have kids.'

While some interviewees mentioned kids changing their behavior,
rather than leading them away from participation in streetlife,
fatherhood simply made them more cautious about their violent
activities. Duff explained, 'I got two kids. Of course I had to change
my way of lifestyle because of them ... worried that they gonna get

hit [by bullets if someone shoots his car], got to protect my kids. You know, touch my kids, I'll get you.' Here, he turned a potential pressure toward desistance into a reason to engage in future violence. Throughout the interview, Duff did little more than claim to be more aware of dangers when his kids were around. Icy Mike, discussing a specific example of why he didn't retaliate against someone who had wronged him, said, 'I got two kids, I can't be locked up in the banger [jail] for that shit.' However, as shown elsewhere in the interview, Icy Mike did nothing to disengage from streetlife and its associated demands of violence. Jaymoon connected the demands of fatherhood and the potential costs of criminal activity to broader mainstream aspirations for his children: 'I got too much to lose ... I got two boys, you know, and that's what I'm living for, living for my boys. That's all I'm trying to do, make it better for them ... I want them to come up here and go to [university] and shit.' Yet nothing in his interview indicated that Jaymoon had done anything concrete to work toward this goal.

As with Duff, several fathers mentioned children and their relationships in the context of potential or actual retaliation carried out for wrongs against them. As discussed in Chapter 4, CrazyJay, talking about his retaliation against someone who had robbed him – taking money and drugs but also a ring he had bought for his infant son – highlighted the injury to his child as a key motivator for his violence: 'Now I'm gonna kill you, not only [for] taking from me, you taking from my kids so now you got to die.' Bishop[12] discussed how he and members of his neighborhood used vigilante justice to protect all of the children in his neighborhood:

There is no outside gang influence in our school district ... but ... if that happened we [his male friends in the neighborhood] were supposed to clean it up ... those kids at those schools are easily influenced and one of these guys in these gangs might have to be only 17 and I would not want any little kids not going home to their mothers, and I definitely didn't want any little kid getting involved in any felony crimes ... I refuse to sell crack, crank, any of that crap to any little kids ... It's about keeping that kind of element from infesting our neighborhood.

While a unique case in the sample,[13] Bishop seemed to be enacting the 'old head' role that Anderson (1999) identifies as a central pillar of African-American communities. Bishop presented his violence as more of a product of social institutional disintegration than spurred by criminal activities and deep embeddedness in streetlife. Bishop's violence was driven by the need to protect his family and community in the absence of structural social control mechanisms (e.g. the police).

Questions about family were generally absent from the interview protocols in the studies drawn upon here; yet the men interjected discussions of their children and female blood relatives into their discussions far more than they did their wives or romantic partners. This suggests that the men saw such relationships as much more central and salient to their daily lives. Even if it was all talk with little action behind it, the fact that the men brought up concerns surrounding their children[14] highlighted this as a crucial element of their masculine identity constructions. Additionally, their discussions of acting as protectors of their female relatives – contrasted with the absence of these discussions related to female street associates – highlights both the contradictory categorization of women into variant cognitive categories and the nature of gendered behavioral expectations toward these different types of women.

Conclusions

Exploring the nature and dynamics of inter-gender interactions on the streets highlights the extreme misogyny embedded within streetlife culture and norms. Men deeply involved in criminal activity held very low opinions of women in general, typically dismissing them as unimportant and insignificant. This was both a producer and a product of the powerful gender segregation in streetlife-dominated neighborhoods. Yet men maintained ties to women in their family networks and were compelled by the same set of masculinities to protect and defend female kin. This created a set of dialectical relationships in which men are dismissive, domineering, and exploitive of some women but protective of others and bound by kinship ties to exact revenge upon men who dominated or exploited their female blood relatives. Women they interacted with as peers were typically seen as little more than tools. Interaction with them was used to satisfy sexual desire and generate masculine capital (see Chapters 3 and 4). Additionally, these women were also used in the completion of criminal enterprises, primarily by acting as decoys to set men up for violent victimization.

Despite these perceptions and actions, the same men saw it as their duty to be protective of their mothers, sisters and female cousins. As one man's 'whore' is another man's sister (or mother), a man who discussed exploiting a woman on the streets during one part of an interview would later discuss assaulting someone who did the same to a female relative of his. Thus these gender relations sparked much masculinity inspired conflict between men on the streets. These contradictory definitions of women – and the contradictory demands that surrounded appropriate treatment of them – framed most inter-gender interactions and motivated many examples of the intra-gender violence.

Treatment of women was not the only contradiction within the enactment of masculinity on the streets of Saint Louis. There were other points of disagreement on proper enactment of street masculinity, in reference to how men should interact with other men and how they should interact with women. Most of these contradictions focus on the nature and enactment of violence. Chapter 6 examines these contradictions in defining, enacting and actualizing masculinities.

Notes

1 With regard to whether women were an acceptable target of violence, many men further expressed sexist and derisive attitudes toward women. However, the language used to describe violence against women was strongly disconnected from the actualities of the behavior. It will be dealt with in Chapter 6.

2 Most of the interviews included questions eliciting examples of offenses not carried out.

3 None of the women in the sample offered such stories, though this is most likely due to the interviews' focus on their own violence.

4 TC described his brother's execution a few lines earlier in the interview. Missouri did not execute anyone between the years of 1966 and 1988. The first lethal injection execution in the state occurred in 1989. There is no indication in the interview that TC lived anywhere else than Saint Louis during his life. At the time of the interview in 2003, TC was 26, therefore not alive in 1972. It is possible his brother was executed in another state, but 1972 is the year the *Furman v. Georgia* decision was handed down by the U.S. Supreme Court that halted executions in the United States. It is possible the execution occurred before the decision, but the first execution by lethal injection in the United States did not occur until 1982, in Texas (Beiser 2005). However, the assault that TC described not retaliating for here involved a head wound requiring 22 stitches. TC admitted that after that injury, 'To this day my memory ain't been the same since.'

5 Despite multiple, lengthy interviews, this is the only mention of Red's child other than the stock interview question of 'How many kids do you have?' Red had three children at the time of the interview.

6 Reinforcing above points about the marginality of wives and girlfriends, although Bishop was one of the few married men in the sample and he frequently discussed his bonds to his blood relatives and the community, he never mentioned his wife and child.

7 These women were not non-violent in their daily lives; they were frequently violent toward other women (even going so far as to exact violence upon a woman at the request of a man – see Mullins, Wright and Jacobs 2004). However, most of the women cited issues of size and strength as the reason they would not engage in violence against men.

8 Although Pooh Bear discussed this as a prostitution incident, when she drew upon the help of her male peers she did not suggest that they needed to exact revenge for her because they were her pimps. Rather, she only suggested a bond of mutual cooperation between herself and the men who assisted her.

9 Having only one child was the modal response (26), with two children being the second most frequent response (15), 14 claimed to have three or more children (with six being the largest number), and 26 (30.2%) reported having no children (five cases (5.8%) had no mention either way of parental status).

10 Not surprisingly, within the context of the interviews, only one mention of the relationship between an interviewee and his father came up. When asked if he would tell anyone about having committed a crime, Smokedog explained, 'I tell my daddy. "Hey I just robbed this cat" ... I be proud of it I guess. He be like, "Well, show [me], let me have some money." I'll give him some money. We be cool.'

11 Alternatively, it could be argued that these were simply neutralization techniques (an 'appeal to higher loyalties' per Sykes and Matza 1957). Yet, the fact that they were framed within the larger demands of masculinity is still significant.

12 Bishop's use of violence seemed less connected to drugs, reputation, or other more typical motivations, and more directed toward the protection of those he cared about. However, his violence was no less severe than other incidents described in the sample.

13 Because of the nature of the snowball sampling procedures used in data collection, non-criminal social networks are under-represented, if not absent, in the data sets used here. Bishop's motivations for violence are unique among these interviews, but they may not be unique within the communities the interviewees live in.

14 Even with careful analysis, it is not possible to say if the men here exhibit these tendencies more strongly toward sons over daughters, or vice versa.

Chapter 6

Is it smart or just a punk ass move? Contradictions of street masculinity

Some early work in the sociology and criminology of gender presented gender norms and roles as monolithic, static structures. Gender was generally approached from the notion that specific behavioral demands of masculinity and femininity were unitary and diametrically opposed. As discussed in Chapter 1, theorizing on gender has advanced considerably. Gender is now understood as dynamic, with multiple masculinities and femininities present in any social context. The fluidity of gender presents numerous problems for 'doing gender' as competing values and behavioral demands make gendered actions rife with role strains (see Goode 1960), problematic and contradictory interpretations of behavior. With regard to street masculinity, many of these problems have been touched upon in previous chapters. This chapter explores these contradictions in more detail. They arose not only from competing definitions of appropriate masculine behavior, but also from diverging opinions of what idealized masculinities demand and what is practical for survival on the streets in specific situations.

Contradictions within street masculinity generally fall into two realms: those relating to the use of violence against men, and those related to the use of violence against women. With regard to men, contradictory definitions often boiled down to a tension between maintaining an image of masculinity on the streets and practical issues in the enactment of violent episodes. However, the most complex set of contradictions emerged when men discussed the use of violence against women in a street context, especially in a retaliatory context. Out of direct questions, probes and general narrative examination, numerous rules and contingencies to those rules arose. This chapter explores the nature of and tensions within contradictions of street masculinity enactment.

Image versus enactment

Sneakiness

As discussed in Chapter 3, men interviewed often defined sneakiness – using the element of surprise to carry out a criminal victimization – as 'punk' behavior. Men who avoided a straight-up fight, attempted to hide their identities when engaged in criminal behavior, sought to avoid violence, or sought out others to carry out violence for them were often defined as weak or cowardly. This seeming lack of bravery and toughness was a conceptual cornerstone of subordinated masculinity.

For example, discussing how someone caught him drunk and unaware, CrazyJay characterized the victimization as punk behavior: 'I think that the way that he did it was cowardly, hiding behind shit and catching me while I'm at my lowest, while I'm drunk or whatever, and I wanted to let him know you couldn't get me on my motherfucking worst day.' The fact that CrazyJay had been victimized was an affront to his masculine street identity – he was shown to be unprepared by being caught off-guard. However, instead of internalizing this as a failure on his own part, he defined the offender's behavior as problematic and specifically unmasculine. Such interpretations of events were common among the interviewees, as shown in Chapter 3. Most of the problematic interpretations arose when men used different standards for judging their own behavior from those used to judge the behavior of others. When discussing their own actions, they emphasized aspects of street masculinity that were apparent in their own behavior. When discussing the actions of others, they framed them as examples of 'punkness' to degrade and devalue the masculinity of the men with whom they had conflicts. This was part and parcel of the power hierarchy on the streets, discussed in both Chapters 3 and 4.

Many men framed catching victims unaware and taking advantage of surprise to accomplish a violent retaliation in a positive light. Black described an episode of vengeance in which his modality mirrored his own victimization: 'You get me from behind, you're – I didn't want that kind of shit ... I ... caught him off-guard. I didn't say nothing. There wasn't a word. I did the same fucking thing he did to me but ... I was facing him.' Black highlighted what he saw as a key difference between his behavior and that of his victimizer. For Black, this form of revenge was justified because it mirrored the form of the victimization he experienced. However, he elevated his own masculinity accomplishment through emphasizing that although he did use surprise to strike at his target, he did it face to face instead of from behind.

Don Love discussed an incident that unveiled contradictions surrounding whether to offer a victim a 'fair fight' or to get the drop on him. Explaining how he handled himself and his business on the streets, Don Love said, 'When you move you gotta move like a thief in the night ... because the *real* bad boys, they hit hard and move silent ... that's *real* G shit ... it's best for motherfuckers to not know what you do.' Yet later in the interview, he castigated someone for laying low and avoiding a violent retaliation:

He's done some cowardly scams and he kind of trying to like, going into a little shell ... trying to hide behind his people ... Street don't like those kind of [people] ... You gotta do [it] very smart in a smart sense ... There's a lot of people know the deal ... if I ... [have] ... to move ... within the range of shit happening 'cause if I let shit die down ... [there would] be ... second guessing – who did this?

Don Love then immediately reemphasized that, 'you don't want anyone to know what you do'.

Like Don Love, many of the men highlighted their own sneaky behavior in carrying out victimizations. They described it as a positive reflection of their street smarts and criminal success. Smokedog presented his sneakiness as a valued and necessary trait: 'I'm too sneaky ... I creep. I creep. I just fuck them back anytime I want to, anytime ... I could just chill in front of your house, two, three o'clock in the morning ... with my seat laid all the way back. Just pull the radio dial real low and I'll just get high, me and my little partner ... you pull up drunk and shit ... get your ass.' Here, Smokedog lauded laying low and catching his target unaware – the precise behavior that Black and CrazyJay denigrated – as an affirmation of his criminal ingenuity.

Many of the interviewees emphasized the practical value of this behavior. Kilo explained, 'I'm a little guy so I hit him when he had his back turned. Just smack him with the butt of the gun, you know, in the back of the head somewhere.' TC offered a counter-definition of 'sneaky' victimizations and the value of being labeled a 'punk': 'See, the thing about it is, the punks, most of the punks and the sneaky people who do it behind your back are the ones which live to tell it. And the cocky ones ... those ones are dead and in jail right now.'

The following exchange between an interviewer and Red also illustrates this perception. As discussed in Chapter 4, Red carried out a lethal retaliation against a man who had slapped his face in a club – presumed retaliation for Red bumping into him and spilling his drink on the man. After being slapped, Red waited outside in the parking lot for the man to emerge and crept up behind him, armed with a pistol:

Interviewer: Wouldn't you want to confront the guy in front of his face like, 'You, you slapped me, nobody slaps me, you're gonna pay?'

Red: No ... when you do stuff like that there ... [you] give [him] the option ... to break back into the car ... he can get a chance to break out and start running. When you sneak up behind him and you hit him once, bang, he gonna spin around. So when he spin around he gonna see you.

Interviewer: Where'd you aim that first shot at?

Red: In the back of the head.

Clearly, Red did not give the man a chance to spin around and see who had shot him. His first shot was purposefully lethal.

'Masking up'

Another point of disagreement within the data was whether it was best to expose or hide one's identity during a violent retaliation. Prior chapters described the need to establish and maintain a street reputation. As Lafonz said, 'Everybody gotta kind of pronounce their manhood.' However, doing so required limiting what one said and to whom, to eliminate the possibility of violent reprisals and police attention. In addition to issues of sneakiness, there was also the consideration of whether to have one's identity as a perpetrator known to either the victim or the community.

One issue raised was whether offenders attempted to disguise their identities with masks when they carried out violent retaliations. The following exchange was typical of why men said they did not wear masks or conceal their identity during a retaliation event:

Interviewer: Were you masked up? …
Jaymoon: No …
Interviewer: Why?
Jaymoon: To let him know. You fucking with the wrong person, simple as that.

Here, hiding his identity would defeat the very purpose of the violent event: exacting revenge and building a reputation as someone not to be 'messed with'. When asked why he didn't wear a mask during his retaliation for the victimization discussed above, CrazyJay explained:

I want to let him know you couldn't get me on my motherfucking worst day. I gave up that easily because you had a gun and I'm smart, I used my head. But I also want to let you know there is consequences and I'm the motherfucker that you took from and I'm the motherfucker that gonna discipline [you for it].

Here, not being masked was highlighted as a specific counter to being caught unaware to begin with. CrazyJay described his retaliation so as to elevate his own masculinity in light of how he was victimized. This was further reinforced by his recourse to the connotations inherent in his use of the word 'discipline': it was something a superior did to a subordinate.

Goldie distinctly linked not hiding his identity to building and enhancing his reputation as both a man and someone who had street credibility:

When you do things uncovered [without a mask] it's like your rank gets more powerful … It's like now you might stand there Super OG … you get more and more prominent. If you're covering up it's like you're a bitch, you don't want them to see who you is. You know, that's bitch stuff. We don't do it like that. We don't do no drive-bys. We do walk-bys or bike-bys … so they can see who we are. We want them to know who it is … I'm gonna let you know who I am. Like I might tell you my name while I'm doing it to you, let you know, 'cause you done it to me or your people's done it to me.

Being identifiable was presented here as crucial in reputation-building; hiding your identity was clearly assigned to subordinate masculinity. For Red, wearing masks was not a concern: 'I don't wear masks ... 'cause anybody I shoot right now, they're dead.' There was indeed a strong element of masculine bravado behind his statement, but the actions he chose to discuss in his interviews backed up his claim.

Despite the framing of identity explored above, many of the men discussed wearing masks while offending and framed the behavior as something positive and practical. Despite his critique of sneaky practices (noted earlier), Black explained why he wore masks during his retaliatory offending:

> I don't want everyone to know my business. They might fucking see me somewhere another time. Saint Louis ain't that big ... you got to play it smart 'cause remember if you rob somebody without a mask on, if you ain't gonna take their life they gonna look around one day and piss the fuck off. Let you have it. Ain't no way [I am] stupid enough for that.

Sugar concurred: 'Sometimes you don't [wear a mask] because that ain't good. If you let them know who you are they gonna come back and get you.' One reason for the divergence in the data over whether to 'mask up' while offending was that some of the interviews were collected to understand predatory acquisitive crimes (e.g. drug robbery and carjacking) and others were collected to illuminate non-acquisitive predatory crimes (e.g. criminal retaliation). All activities were embedded within the structures of streetlife broadly and street masculinity specifically, but the overarching purpose of the two types of violence were distinctly different. In the former, the major purpose was the acquisition of goods (money, drugs, vehicles, etc.); in the latter, the purpose was revenge. That said, the discussions quoted here were focused not on robbery but on retaliation. As Jacobs (2000) has explored, robbery itself functions as a form of retaliation on the streets.

To summarize, the enactment of street violence, especially that driven by the enhancement of masculine reputation, contained contradictions surrounding whether one fulfilled the express demands of constructing a tough street image or attended to issues of practicality during the violent episode. Getting the drop on someone and wearing a mask during the event were labeled as both 'punk' and smart. No clear-cut lines appeared in the data; sometimes the same man had contradictory takes on events. In general, it seemed to be reducible to the interviewee framing the behavior (whatever it was) in a way that enhanced his masculinity and devalued others' masculinity.

Using proxies to accomplish retaliation

Another contradiction emerged when men discussed having others either carry out a retaliation for them or drew upon others for assistance in retaliating. Many of the men insisted that if someone had wronged them on the streets and they didn't respond personally, then they had lost key masculine capital. The following exchange, first noted in Chapter 3, between Goldie and an interviewer highlighted this point:

Interviewer: Have you ever gotten someone else to retaliate for you?

Goldie: Not at all … [I] don't want them to. When I got shot my nephew was out there going crazy, calling up saying 'What do you want me to do?' 'I want you to do nothing' … It was done to me you know, like it might be somebody do something to my nephew. Most likely he not gonna want me to jump in, he gonna want to do everything on his own, so if he do the crime he do the time, you know. Ain't no use everybody doing the time.

Goldie offered up two reasons for avoiding the use of proxies: (1) the desire to exact his own revenge; and (2) the more realistic realization that if he handled his business on his own, others would not be legally culpable for the actions.

Black's discussion of why he would never use a proxy was similarly grounded in core elements of street masculinity: 'I take care of myself … Why spend the money for it? … I got a few little homies out there who would do something. You know, I got some that would do something for free for me but then I'd have to owe them and I don't want to do that.' Here the crucial element was not the protection of his peers but the obligation and debts that relying upon them would generate. Such ties conflicted with street masculinity ideals about independence and freedom from such ties.

Nonetheless, some of the men admitted to using, or being used as, proxies to carry out a retaliation. Typically, men who discussed incidents when they acted as proxies described incidents that revolved around family members who had been victimized. The interviewees took it upon themselves to avenge a family member who was either incapacitated (e.g. in hospital) or could not personally find the individual in question.

Contradicting Goldie's insistence that he took care of the above-mentioned retaliation on his own, his older brother DL, in a separate interview, claimed to have attempted to orchestrate the mandated vengeance. 'He [the victim] happened to hit my little brother Goldie … We just waited … Anybody that was out there got shot … I tried to get him [the man who shot his brother] … He [the victim] didn't [care] about who got hit [when he shot my brother].' In another incident, DL admitted to carrying out a retaliation for someone else as the intended victim 'would have been expecting him [the man for whom DL served as a proxy]'. DL, however, could easily get the drop on the intended victim, thereby successfully carrying out payback.

As with DL, many other men claimed to have carried out retaliations for members of their family. Icy Mike described how he took retaliation for the death of his uncle: 'His [Icy Mike's uncle] baby's mama stabbed him a couple of weeks before he got shot … I think the bitch shot him … I beat her ass because I know she had something to do with it. She was the only motherfucker that was close to him like that … That's the only thing I could do.' Such retaliations were grounded in the tenets of street masculinity's demands to protect one's family. In addition to these positive discussions of acting as a proxy for a family member, other men framed the use of a proxy in any violent encounter as a positive reflection on their masculinity.

For some of the men, the use of proxies indicated their elevated position on the streets. After discussing being robbed, Don Love explained why he didn't see it as necessary to exact revenge for himself: 'I didn't get tripped off of it [being robbed] because I was gonna send some [of my] OG homies. I know they [the robbers] was gonna grind down on me anyway 'cause they was from a 'hood that they [his peers] didn't like.' E also provided an example of this approach. When asked if he had ever used others to retaliate for him, he responded, 'I've been in a situation like that before. If you can't find them, then I send my forces out there.' Elaborating on a specific incident, he continued, 'I had some of my boys beat him [a man whom he could not find] down and put him in the hospital, break his legs.' When asked why he didn't do it himself, E stated, 'I don't like to get my hands dirty. I don't have to get my hands dirty when I got forces. When I got boys who want to do it … They do it [for free].' Icy Mike similarly had no problem using the assistance of others, also framing some retaliation as beneath him: 'I didn't want to get my hands dirty, you dig? ... I don't want to be branded with no motherfucking killing.' Note Icy Mike's additional pragmatism in avoiding a serious criminal charge as a result of his actions.

Along these lines, Paris allowed his family members to retaliate for him because he 'didn't want to take the blame, 'cause the police already had my name or whatever, you know, 'cause they picked me up from the ambulance or whatever and I know they just gonna be like "maybe this guy did it" or whatever ... I'm on probation now so I just kinda chill out. If I really want to remain static like that I'd have to get somebody else to do it.' Feeling pressure from the police, Paris saw it as most practical to avoid further personal involvement.

Further highlighting the contradictions at play, Don Love explained why he didn't use proxies, despite his earlier discussions of how proxies enhanced his street status: 'The thing is, I don't want it to happen. I want to be the guy that takes them on ... this the one, this one who disrespected me ... [It's] personal.' It was not clear from Don Love's interview what specifically would make something personal as compared to 'business'.

Broad expectations of street masculinity required that men respond to slights, yet a number provided numerous examples of *not* responding to violence with violence. Many of the men simply said they had yet to retaliate because they had been unable to find the perpetrator. Others provided rationales for letting the incident 'slide'. This is notable because letting an incident slide was potentially 'punk' behavior that would need to be legitimated by the offenders to avoid a loss of face. One typical reason for not responding to slights with violence was that the offender was a close friend or family member. Kow described an incident involving a close friend who pulled a gun on him over a woman. Kow's friend walked into the apartment that the friend shared with the woman to find her and Kow alone. The man got angry and pulled a gun on Kow. Kow diffused the potential violence by leaving, but the mere act of being threatened with a gun was a serious challenge. Explaining why he did nothing in response to the threat, Kow said, 'He was a friend of mine. I grew up with him ... He come down, used to be my partner ... His girl, all his family, we all grew up together in the same street ... He has to lead his life.'

Similarly, Big Mac offered the same reference to a friend's fictive kin status as reason for not exacting revenge: 'One of my friends I grew up with and he came to me and said he had some trouble and needed a gun. And I was, like, kind enough to give him a gun. Trust him with it. "Do whatever you gonna do, but bring it back." He didn't bring it back.' As discussed in Chapter 4, theft is an offense that typically requires retaliation on the streets. Big Mac went on to explain why he did not exact revenge in this case:

> I don't know, I was trying to change my ways. I was coming up. So now I'm a grown man, ain't no kid no more … I see him all the time. I grew up with him in the same neighborhood … Another thing that made me leave it alone was his mama. She came, she paid me for it, even though I didn't want no money, I wanted my gun back.

As discussed in earlier chapters, theft was an offense that often required response; not doing so could brand one on the streets as an easy mark. Through making reference to his own maturation processes (e.g. trying to change his ways, not being a kid any more) as well as personal ties between him, the man who borrowed the gun, and the man's mother, Big Mac offered contingencies within the hegemony of masculine violence on the streets.

Jaymoon described a similar situation, though the theft was more severe. After a friend had stolen drug money from him, Jaymoon tried to get the money back, to no avail. He then explained how he responded to the theft: 'I just stopped messing with him. I hoped he'd be having a nice night with it, except that he won't be able to do it no more 'cause I stopped messing with him.' By cutting the man off from a drug supply, Jaymoon prevented a future victimization. He also provided a detailed explanation for why he chose not to engage in more severe retaliatory violence against his former friend: 'This is one of my partners I grew up with … He got bills, I got bills, we all got bills. He got kids … I just stopped messing with him. I left it alone. I took it as a loss. His mama is like my mama, my mama is like his mama.' Again, social networks of fictive kin dissuaded potential violence.

One additional case explored how family connections and ties diffused a violent situation. Darnell described being set up for a violent victimization that left him hospitalized. However, once healthy, he did not exact payback:

> The only reason I didn't do nothing to them is because of their grandmother. They was taking care of they granny. I'm a

granny's boy myself. If I would have taken on them boys she probably wouldn't be here … wouldn't have lived. That's the only reason I didn't. She talked to me and talked to me. She was at the hospital every day.

Through invoking the protective and chivalric functions of masculinity, Darnell reframed his lack of retaliation as something positive, yet still distinctly masculine in nature.

The rules of violence against women

One of the most central sets of contradictions in the data revolve around whether it was acceptable to use violence against women. Further, if it was acceptable, when was violence allowed and what form should it take? Masculine discourses about women on the streets highlighted women's marginalized status and their lack of importance to men deeply embedded in streetlife. Such frameworks of subordination generated demands for protection, leniency and typically ignoring challenges and slights delivered by women. According to the interviewees, women on the street simply were not dangerous enough to elicit serious consideration and response. Such attitudes generated discourses suggesting that men should never be violent with a woman. Yet women frequently experience violence by men through all segments of the US social structure, and the streets are no exception.

Much of the following discourse was derived from a single question offered up to male informants during the retaliation study: would you ever retaliate against a woman? As the following shows, this question tended to produce a negative response; men denied that they did or would do such a thing, for a number of reasons detailed below. However, once probed, many of the men admitted to drawing upon violence to negotiate their relationships with women. This highlighted a contradiction within their patriarchal worldview that often sent them into a set of cognitive gymnastics as they tried to justify their use of violence in a specific case with broader norms that suggested that violence against women was a distinctly 'punk move'.

Non-violence

One perspective emerging from the men's discussions of women and violence was an adamant denial that they should take such measures with a woman, no matter what she has done. Kow made the issue seem black and white: 'Don't get into it with a woman … She just gonna talk … A woman can't do no harm to you.' Play Too Much similarly saw women as unimportant, as they really posed no threat to him: 'No, I don't believe in hitting women. I mean, I'm not gonna just let a woman put her hands on me, that's petty. It's mind over matter. Once a man puts his foot down, a woman understands. I mean I don't … hit women or retaliate against women.' However, this vague reference to using a minimal level of violence to 'put his foot down' left unclear exactly what this meant.

Icy Mike gendered his discussion here, saying that if a woman ever wronged him, 'I don't want to knock her off the block 'cause that's a woman and shit … I want it to be a man and shit so I can get on the motherfucker's head.' The implication was that he could truly extract necessary revenge on a man, but women were out of bounds for more serious violence. Duff also denied that he would ever strike a woman, yet a potential contingency crept into his explanation: 'Never … it would have to depend on what's going on because I was always raised not to hit a woman, no matter what. I always live by that. My mother was a strong woman so I live by that, but if it ever came down to it I don't know how I would react … never had to hit a woman.' Many of the men here provided such qualifications; the use of violence against women, generally seen as something to be avoided (or at least to avoid talking about), was acceptable under certain conditions (see also Miller and White 2003). Speezy provided an example of this when he described when a man did use violence against a woman, though Speezy himself did not. He explained:

Women … try to fuck you up. [With] a man you just go the whole nine [yards] … 'cause he's gonna try to hurt you … I know women who have set people up. Matter of fact the girl I was messing with, her cousin was messing with my friend. They were in a hotel. She stole his car. So he bust her head in … I did not bust her head in, he did. I don't deal with women like that.

Unpacking these contingencies is the focus of the remainder of this chapter.

Alternative targets

Some of the men indicated that they would not get physically violent with a woman when she had wronged him, but they would not simply ignore the slight. Rather, they would direct their violence at another target. TDog discussed a situation in which a woman had wronged him by not paying him back money – something that could have produced serious violence had she been a man:

> She owed me some money and she ran off with my money and when I got to her I just basically shook her down, roughed her up a bit but I didn't punch her, though. Men, their word it's all you can go by but [a woman is] just a woman. I wouldn't want nobody doing nothing to no female in my family … If there was a woman that owed me lots of money, I will, you know, retaliate on her hardware or car, anything, house [but not her person].

While TDog did use violence, he was careful to insist that he 'didn't punch' the woman, drawing a parallel with his own likely response if someone had done such a thing to a member of his family. Rather, he indicated that there are other, more appropriate targets for exacting vengeance on women – their property. Goldie offered the same alternative for retaliating against women:

> I don't go around busting up women or shit like that. Nor pull no gun on them … Bitch might fuck my car up. So I'd retaliate and fuck her car up … It [beating her up] ain't even worth it. You know I wouldn't want no motherfucker beating on my little sisters or little cousins and shit. I do it to man. A man can handle that. Women can't.

Goldie echoed TDog's sentiments about not wanting something similar to happen to members of his family, and in doing so highlighted broader masculinity codes on the streets. Additionally, he further gendered these ideas by forthrightly attributing these differences to perceptions of innate toughness and abilities of men to withstand such violence (making it allowable) and the innate inability of women to do so (thereby making it off-limits).

Geasy explained that if he were wronged by a woman he would target a male romantic partner of hers:

> I mean, a girl can't hurt you know unless you let her … There's some scandalous girls but if you showed them what you can do to a motherfucker then they'll change it, they just be cool … 'I'm gonna pop your boy right now. Pop his ass and you don't

want that to happen to you.' Call her back the next day and tell
her, 'What you think about what happened yesterday?'

Although he started off with the assertion that women 'can't hurt
you', Geasy quickly qualified this to indicate that there were indeed
violent, 'scandalous' women on the streets. However, the best way to
control them was through their male partners.

Using female proxies

Among the men who insisted that they would never use violence
against a woman, some were not willing to simply allow women's
slights to slide. Instead of exacting revenge themselves, a common
response was to have a woman handle any violence the man wished
to visit upon the woman. Dub provided a clear example of this: 'I
don't hit females. Well, I can't say that. I could get another female
to hit her.' When asked if he would ever violently retaliate against a
woman, TD explained:

> No. [I] always have my girlfriend handle a woman … The girls
> like, you know, you got girls in your family … If I get involved
> with a girl I'd get a girl, the girls would take care of it and [if]
> they have trouble with the boys, then we go help them out …
> You got women [to] take care of women, you got men taking
> care of men … Me, myself, would feel less of a man retaliating
> on a female so I feel like you have to be equal so if it was a
> male it would be a whole different thing.

Not only did TD indicate that this was behavior designed to protect his
own masculine sense of self, he indicated that a gendered reciprocity
existed within his social networks. V-O described a similar pattern:
'Have I retaliated against a woman? No, I get my niece and other
girls to do that … I don't like dealing with women … You don't
ever want to touch them … Anyone ever touch my mother or my
girl [and I would hurt them] … that's just how I was brought up.
Taught never to touch a woman.' By using women to exact revenge
on other women, men avoided the problematic aspects of using
violence against unacceptable targets. At the same time, it allowed
them to satisfy the desire to exact vengeance.

In his interviews, Goldie frequently insisted that he was never
violent with a woman and that he never let someone else handle
his 'business' for him, yet he claimed to have no problem sending

someone else out to resolve an issue for him if the target was a woman:

> 'Cause a woman ain't gonna stand ... I know a woman can't stand it at all like a man could, 'cause I'm probably gonna wanna swing, I'm gonna want to touch you ... I wouldn't even go there. I'd get one of my little homies on the side to get on down with her ... [otherwise] I [would seem] like a bitch [by] whooping a girl or robbing [her], that's going on like a bitch.

Thus, in response to norms that degrade men's use of violence against women, some men draw upon women[1] to maintain their social positions when slighted by a woman. However, some men did get violent with women in a streetlife context. In light of the values that defined such violence as potentially 'punk' behavior, these men offered contingencies that justified the use of violence.

Seriousness of the threat posed by the woman

Despite strongly stated norms that eschew using violence against women, men did indeed use violence as a key tool in their interactions with women. Even some of the men quoted above admitted that there were places, times and reasons to be violent. One justification centered around the severity of the threat the woman posed – if her slight against the man put him in sufficient danger, this allowed a violent reprisal.

While initially insisting that men should never use violence against women, V-O refined his beliefs in this way: 'A woman [would] have to do something very serious for me [to be violent with her] ... I would say if she tried to poison me or ... or [was] setting me up to get hit.' Dub also qualified his more general statements about not hurting women:

> Say she sets me up to get robbed, I can get killed, my people can get hurt and she take something that I earn ... So if you could have killed me I'm most likely gonna kill you [if you are a woman] ... There's like only two things you can get killed for. Trying to kill me or putting me in a position where I could have been killed.

These examples suggested that the threat against the man must be lethal, or nearly so, to elicit violence against a female.

Not as vehement in his denials of avoiding violence against women, Big Mac saw it as necessary only under certain circumstances:

> I don't get no kicks out of putting my hands on a woman, but sometimes a woman would take it too far and she know the right button to push to make you go there – and it's like … I don't think there's no excuse for nothing like that, but by me being who I am … it's all depending on the nature of whatever she done.

Big Mac's comment suggested limitations in the use of violence against women on the street. He indicated it was somewhat unacceptable to do so ('there's no excuse'), but Big Mac clearly indicated that such actions were possible, even probable, under certain conditions.

Smokedog also indicated that it would have to be a specific type of offense to elicit violence against a woman: 'Only way I'd probably do it is if she try to set me up. That's the only way … I've choked a lot of bitches, pushed they heads against walls and shit … they were playing me, man. Bitches got to pay for real. It ain't cool to fuck around … It ain't cool to put a shooter [a gun] at her head.' Smokedog vacillated between disparaging the behavior, expressing intense sexist and violent attitudes, and back to expressing a limit on the type of violence allowable. This fluctuation emphasized the contradictory nature of the rules surrounding violence against women on the streets.

TC's discussion also exhibited vacillation:

> I don't think it is OK [to hit women], but if it is so far as defending yourself, then [it is] OK. What I did [beat up a woman] was totally wrong … I had time to sit down and thought about it and went out there and I did that … Now if she came over and hit me, hit me and hit me, then I just fire up and 'pow, pow' then that's just defending myself, that's totally different, but I don't feel it's OK for a man to hit a woman unless it's truly necessary … Like if you have a woman that's bigger than you … then you just have to … defend yourself. If you got a woman that's just small and hitting you, you get away from her … Get away from her. I don't want to sound like no punk or nothing but try to run … sometimes when you got women just feisty like that, they get off on that and basically … what they need is somebody to knock them down.

TC's discourse shifted from framing hitting women as wrong, even going so far as to admit that he was wrong for beating a woman, to attempting to illustrate circumstances in which it is acceptable. He also highlighted his premeditation when he used such violence, which made the situation more problematic to him. After an altercation in which the woman had hit him a few times, he went home but continued to think about the situation. Then he went back out on the streets, tracked her down, and beat her up. By claiming that men should ignore violence by smaller (and thus weaker) women, TC reaffirmed values that focus on not using violence with women, but he closed with a statement suggesting that violence was required to keep 'feisty' women in line.

Not going 'drastic'

Among the men who discussed being violent with women, most suggested that since, in their view, women are weaker, a man should not use the same severity with a woman that he would with a man. Dub simply said, 'You don't go so drastic on a woman.' Hops concurred, explaining that certain behaviors were allowable, 'like grabbing her, choking her, but [just] so as you don't kill her. Choking her but not kill her … [but against a man I would be] straight up trying to kill him. You be in the process of doing that to a woman, it would be like you kind of feel sorry for her, she's weaker and more defenseless.' Describing such an incident, Big Mac illustrated the contradictory ideals expressed by Dub: 'I just smacked her a couple of times … I smacked a little blood but I ain't got my fists up … I ain't fighting her like no man or nothing like that.'

Jhustle also attempted to clarify the differences in severity of violence used depending on the gender of the target:

'Cause a man is a man … if I'm gonna do a retaliation on a man it's gonna be for some reason and whatever I'm gonna retaliate for, I'm either gonna kill him or I'm gonna disable him somehow … he's gonna be really fucked up … A woman, you know, I'd be more lenient. It just depends on what she do … A woman, they pretty much get away with it … I might pay for somebody to whoop her ass or something … teach her a lesson … There's like a point you have to prove to them, like to get their respect. So you have to be not as hard but you have to be … hard, but kind of soft. Something like hard but firm.

When confronted with their use of violence against women, men who described these activities danced around a presentation of self that affirmed the actions but framed them in such a way to avoid appearing like less of a man. Jhustle's attempt to describe violence that is 'hard' but 'soft' and 'firm' draws attention to the problematic nature of the issue.

Acting like a man

A few men articulated the difference between using violence against women and men in clearly gendered terms. They referred to women *becoming* men when they chose to undertake certain actions. E put the issue in clear language: 'If she can go out there and do the things a man do, *she man enough* to get her[s] like a man.' Women 'earned' honorary masculine status by participating in masculine activities. The following interchange between an interviewer and Kow also brought this to light. Earlier in the chapter, Kow stated that he ignored women because they cannot harm him; when probed on the issue, his views were more complex. While he began by adhering to the earlier statement of women as non-threatening (and thus unworthy of violence), he quickly modified the nature of this belief:

Kow: A woman ain't gonna do nothing to you ... she might just go and get somebody for you, but she won't actually hurt you ... she a woman, she ain't gonna do nothing to you.

Interviewer: There are some women out there who will rob you ... and then what do you do in that situation?

Kow: Oh man, you smack the shit out of her. You smack her fucking ass.

Interviewer: So at that point ... she becomes a man?

Kow: Right ... if she man enough to stick her hand in your pocket, you know it's just like going in your face ... if you *man* enough to stick you hand in, you *man* enough to take the rap.

This conferment of symbolic masculine status was used to justify violence.[2] If a woman was embedded in streetlife and pursued activities defined as masculine, then she removed the protections bestowed on her due to her sex.

Sex as a weapon

As discussed earlier, some of the men described targeting a women's property over their person if she had wronged them. Other men in the sample – especially when responding to slights delivered upon them by women they were romantically involved with – discussed using sexual infidelity as a way to get back at their partners. Geasy said, 'Sex is the way of everything ... This girl, right, I was going with her and her mom wanted to spoil the relationship with her, so I caught her mom by herself and I told her to come over to my house and talk to me, then I fucked her mom and told her [his girlfriend] about it.' While it was unclear from the interviews whether Geasy felt challenged by the woman he was dating, her mother, or both, he acted against both of them.

Jhustle described a time when he used sex to exact payback on a girlfriend who had taken money from him without his permission: 'If a woman fucks with me, takes some money from me ... I try to get people back in the worse way. So if I fuck their cousin or something that will really piss her off, more than that $50.' Through the use of sex, men exacted harm upon women they felt had wronged them. When asked if he would ever use sex as a weapon against a woman, Icy Mike, referring to a current partner, said, 'I would probably go fuck somebody ... I'll get somebody in her family, they digging me anyway.' Red offered a similar discussion in describing how he responded when his current romantic partner was angry with him: 'It's like OK, you mad at me, so I go fuck your partner ... I know your partner liking on me, she digging on me, so I'm gonna go knock your partner off ... instead of beating her down, just play on her mind. Hurt her by fucking with one of her partners.'

TC provided an example of this behavior taken to the extreme, both in how he carried it out and how he let his partner know it had happened. The event was triggered by TC's belief that his girlfriend had cheated on him:

> With this woman, matter of fact, I'm the best thing going for her. I kind of changed her world, but for some reason she feels that ... this [relationship] can't be the cream of the crop, gotta be something better ... out there. So what she did, she went out and messed around and found out that ... there wasn't anybody better than me, and so what happened was I cheated on her with her cousin ... [I made a video tape of the incident] ... Take it [the tape] and played it [for her] ... [I was] doing

extra things I never even done with her ... had her [the cousin] hitting Mariah Carey high notes ... I mean, it pissed her off.

Men saw this as a viable (non-violent) way to control the women in their lives. It evaded norms against physical violence and was presumed to carry more weight due to men's beliefs that women invested more energy in interpersonal relationships than they did.

The latter portion of the criminal retaliation interviews asked men directly if they had ever used sexual assault as a way to exact payback on women who had wronged them. Only one such case emerged.[3] In response to a woman stealing a large amount of drug money from him, V-O orchestrated a group sexual assault on the woman. The woman was invited over to his house, where the men waited. When she arrived, 'Everybody got her ... well, everybody just all took their turn with her.'

When sexual assault was raised, some of the men insisted that men should avoid such behaviors. E explained why he wouldn't sexually assault women who had wronged him: 'You use sex, that's rape. I don't go for that, not in my game. She make you mad, smack her around, but don't rape her. You want to kill her, kill her. Take her out, leave her there ... Killing a woman is better than raping her ... 'cause [with] murder you get a lesser charge. Rape you get a big charge.' Respect for women was clearly not the key factor here, but E's perception of what would bring him more jail time was the primary explanation. Duff provided a similar account:

I think that's [sexual assault] stupid 'cause, I mean, I never been into it but those who have, I mean, I'm pretty sure there was a reason. OK, no woman deserves to be raped, you know, but it could be reasonably a thing that make a person do that. Wrong signs or something ... Like let's say for instance a guy's dating a girl ... they kissing and all that and she says 'No'. OK, to retaliate he's so hyped and he just take it ... Me personally, I feel no woman deserves that but someone [in] some case I would think they would ... Most people wouldn't even try, they'd just say to hell with it. Otherwise you got a serious case on your head and the next thing you know you're in court, she's in court, accusing you of raping her or she'd just lie and say you'd did it.

Like E, Duff emphasized the potential criminal justice consequences of the behavior, but he also assigned a moral element as well. However,

Duff clearly offered up rape myths (see Scully 1990) in explaining why some women would get raped and some men would commit rape.

Conclusions

This chapter has explored some of the key contradictions in the actualization of street masculinity. No set of gender demands (or any other role, for that matter) is clear-cut and easy to accomplish in action. Any set of structural expectations contain contradictory demands. In the hegemonic masculinity seen on the streets of Saint Louis, several key contradictions emerged. The data highlighted numerous points of contention concerning acceptably masculine behaviors. These translated directly into variance in the nature and extent of violence on the streets.

Men on the streets saw reputation as essential; it had to be cultivated and protected. Criminal violence of many sorts was central to this process, but also had many potential costs, including retaliation and imprisonment. The ideology of street masculinity insisted that any attempt to avoid a fight, to take advantage of an opponent's weaknesses, or to hide one's identity was punk behavior. A man 'broadcasted' his manhood on the streets, yet survival and continued success in criminal endeavors required that he avoid divulging too much about those activities; specific knowledge led to unwanted police attention and allowed his victims to find and target him for retaliation. Thus, men walked a fine line navigating these contradictory demands. When asked to discuss or explain their and others' behavior, men emphasized the aspect of street masculinity that was best illustrated by their behavior and whose violation is best exemplified by their antagonists. Men praised their own sneakiness as street-smart and criminally necessary, but disparaged men who got the drop on them by framing that same sneakiness as cowardly and painting them as punks who refused to stand for a fair fight.

When calling on others to retaliate for them, several counter-definitions emerged. Many of the men saw this as a sign of weakness, of being unable to handle their own affairs. Others positioned this as a sign of social power; having people to exact revenge for them indicated an elevated position on the streets. Additionally, in relation to female targets, some of the men saw the use of proxies as a way around the general rules discouraging violence against women; having a woman exact payback allowed them to simultaneously enhance their street reputations by showing others they were not to be messed with, without violating rules about mistreating women directly.

Trying to understand men's use of violence against women demands navigating some contradictory pillars of street masculinity. Men used violence to establish, maintain, and protect their position on the streets. It was a fundamental way in which men responded to challenges and offenses against them. Views of women that defined females as innately weak and thus in need of some measure of protection were deeply ingrained in the ideology of street masculinity. While most interactions within streetlife networks were intra-gender in nature, men and women did interact in a variety of ways. Men found themselves challenged by women and were the targets of female criminality that demanded some form of response. While some men were seemingly undeterred by notions of protection (or by potential retaliation from her male peers and relatives), many men saw it necessary to treat women who had wronged them differently from men who had done so. Whether calling upon female peers to exact payback for them, claiming to be less severe in their use of violence or using non-physically violent means to respond, any response was a delicate negotiation of competing masculine demands.[4]

Earlier work in the area of gender's intersection with crime in general, but masculinity's connections specifically, has dealt with the demands of such gender performances as static and monolithic categories. However, these contradictions emphasize the dynamic and fluid nature not only of gender, but also of gender's intersection with violence. The dual pressures of identity formation and safety were often resolved through protecting oneself first, then, when reconstructing the event for another, finding a way to legitimize that behavior. The broader, theoretical implications of these contradictions for understanding gender and the gendered nature of violence on the streets is explored in the final chapter.

Notes

1 Although Goldie did not indicate the gender of his 'homies' in the above quote, throughout the interview he was insistent about men not using violence against women.

2 While not related to the gender of the target, a few of the men also discussed this same processes with regard to age. If an older boy (e.g. in his teens) was heavily involved in streetlife activities, the usual protections given to him due to his age were also removed.

3 Within the carjacking interviews, one offender mentioned that he and his partner used the threat of rape to procure a woman's vehicle. This was not by design. The interviewee's partner had urinated immediately prior to their approach of the target; he had forgotten to zip up his pants. The female target read this as a threat of sexual assault. While this was not their intent, they did play up the perceived threat to accomplish the carjacking. Another interviewee in the carjacking sample mentioned selecting a target because he wanted the woman's vehicle and because he wanted her. He did not expressly mention sexually assaulting her.

4 Left unaddressed here, primarily due to the absence of such incidents in the data, is the question of domestic violence against romantic partners or spouses. While there are some hints of this in the data (e.g. men saying that they 'put their foot down' with a woman and there are no more problems), the more strongly represented discussions of men's outright dismissal of these women as unimportant to them left many potential incidents undisclosed. If these types of violence had been explored more thoroughly by the data collectors, this issue may have been clarified or further obfuscated by contradictions.

Chapter 7

Masculinities, streetlife and violence

The goal of this book has been to identify, explore and explain the interconnections of masculinities and violence on the streets of an economically depressed rust-belt city. Drawing upon secondary analysis of previously collected interviews with 110 active offenders (86 men, 24 women), this project has primarily attempted to define the contours of street masculinity and understand how its gendered ideologies produce and support violence on the streets of Saint Louis, Missouri. Using feminist theorizations of masculinities as dynamic and fluid, I have shown how men's (and women's) perceptions and expectations of male violence are inextricably linked to notions of proper *maleness*. While there are other motivations and influences that contribute to the overall production of street violence as a social phenomenon, gender frames, molds, and interprets these events.

In Chapter 1, I raised some critical questions regarding the current understanding of the intersection of gender and criminal offending – specifically those related to the influence and interconnections of masculinities and violence. The field of criminology has long identified violence as the general purview of men. Early work exploring street violence *in situ* identified maleness and masculine reputation as key aspects and focal concerns behind these activities (e.g. Cohen 1955; Miller 1958). Recent work has framed men's use of violence as developing out of and constituting a key pillar of masculinity (for example, see Adler and Polk 1996; Connell 1987, 1995; Messerschmidt 1993, 2000; Newburn and Stanko 1994). Most recent work on masculinities and violence, however, has been either primarily theoretical in nature, with little in the way of systematic examination of empirical data, or too narrowly focused on masculinity as a monolithic, static set of social expectations. The field has recently seen excellent qualitative work elucidating the complexities of gender's relationship to offending when working with female offenders (e.g. Maher 1997; Miller 1998, 2001). Such work has highlighted the intricate and nuanced manner in which gender influences women offenders, yet few works in this vein have focused on men. Within a US context, those that have (e.g. Messerschmidt 2000) have been done with very small samples, focusing more on case studies than on systematic explorations. This study, which draws on a much larger sample containing both men and women, attempts to rectify this key absence.

Chapter 2 discussed the nature of the combined sample used here, emphasizing that when exploring such seemingly omnipresent issues as gender, secondary analysis of previously collected data can serve as an excellent tool for the general explorations of the phenomenon in question. While most of the interviews here were collected without issues of gender at the forefront (or even with any questions about gender contained within them), gendered meanings were so strong in the minds of the social actors that gender came to the surface even when not directly elicited. In fact, except for some of the discussions of men's use of violence against women on the streets, all issues related to masculinity arose out of discussions stimulated by questions directly focused on phenomenological aspects of offending (e.g. motivation, enactment and goods disposal). Only about 25 of the interviews in the criminal retaliation study asked questions about gender directly; these questions were similarly phenomenological but directly queried the respondents about inter-gender retaliatory violence.

In some ways, this study began as a gamble over whether the data would strongly represent the issues of interest. Earlier work had shown that this sort of inquiry was potentially fruitful (e.g. Miller 1998; Mullins and Wright 2003), but those projects drew upon datasets that were in many ways richer in detail than some of the samples used here (e.g. the drug robbery, carjacking and snitching samples). Notably, gender was so at the forefront in the minds and actions of many of the interviewees that in most areas of inquiry here the data were rich and strong. In some ways, the findings discussed in the preceding chapters are even more remarkable as the gendered worldview of the interviewees was not an expressed concern of the data gathering processes. Overall, the findings show the value of this approach; the work here is a methodological testament to the productivity of secondary analysis of qualitative data. For reasons discussed in Chapter 2, such analytical approaches are rarely used in qualitative studies; I hope studies such as this one will act as a catalyst for future interest in this method and allow existing qualitative data sets to be put to much more extensive use.

Chapter 3 explored the nature of street masculinity in Saint Louis – the hegemonic form of masculinity that emerged in the data. Masculinity does not sit within social structure as a monolithic set of static role demands and behavioral expectations. Rather, any social location produces multiple masculinities that are defined in relation to each other (as well as in relation to femininities – see Connell 1987, 1995). Street masculinity is defined by heightened sensitivity to issues of personal reputation. It is enacted through displays of independence from others, self-control, and power over others. These broad demands are intensified by a distinct lack of trust of anyone else on the streets and a profound sense of fatalism. These characteristics undergird the use of violence in establishing and maintaining one's self-identity and street reputation as a man.

Street masculinity is defined, and elevated as hegemonic, in relation to subordinate masculinities and femininities on the street corner. The key subordinate masculinity that emerged out of the men's discourses was that of 'punk': a feminized man who could not adhere to or actualize the stringent demands of street masculinity.[1] 'Punk' was a term frequently used to describe (and define) men who could not physically defend themselves (or their families) against violence, who were neither tough nor a perceived threat to men actualizing street masculinity. The term was also used to describe people frequently selected as targets of violence – especially violence that was acquisitive (e.g. targets for drug robberies or carjackings). For example, men would say they decided to rob a dealer because he 'looked like a punk'. Alternatively, one's response to a violent victimization could 'earn' them the appellation of punk, and once the label spread, it cast them as easy marks for future offending by the interviewees and their peers. In one aspect, then, much of street masculinity's insistence on violence as a response to personal slights was framed as a way of avoiding being labeled a punk.

While many aspects of street masculinity are also found in more mainstream constructions of maleness (e.g. toughness, independence, self-sufficiency), the way in which the men actualized these perceived demands departed significantly from masculinity performances in other social locations. When comparing street masculinity's demands with those of more mainstream identities, it elevates the sensitivity one has toward interpersonal slights and centralizes the use of violence as a key element in gender identity creation and reinforcement well beyond adolescence and early adulthood, though, as some excellent British work has shown, some masculinities maintain these foci into older age grades as well (see Collison 1996; Hobbs 1994; Hobbs *et al.* 2003; Williams and Taylor 1994; Winlow 2001). This specific configuration makes sense in light of the absence of other, more mainstream, masculine capital such as education and work typically used to construct middle-class gender identities. The racial composition (and racial experiences) of the sample further intensified this lack of capital.

Work on intersectionality suggests that socioeconomic class and race/ethnicity are crucial social contexts that interact with gender to (re)define masculinities (or femininities) within a given social location (e.g. Simpson and Elis 1995; Messerschmidt 1993, 1997). However, the interviewees here had no variation within race/ethnicity: they were all African-American. Additionally, there was little variation in terms of socio-economic class; per Gilbert's (1998) model, essentially all respondents at the time of the interview were underclass, with potentially a quarter of them being working poor.[2] Thus, without the ability to compare cases within the sample, it was not possible to make strong statements about the influence of race/ethnicity and socio-economic class on gender as examined here.

That said, the findings here suggest that mainstream masculinities are refracted in the context of concentrated racialized urban poverty. Experiencing the double jeopardy of racial discrimination and the lack of economic opportunities severely reduced the social and gender capital available to these men to construct a masculine identity. It is in this context that violence emerged as a vehicle for accumulating masculine capital. Violence, both acquisitive and non-acquisitive, served as an essential social tool used to define street masculinity as well as subordinate masculinities and femininities. *Real* men are simultaneously aware of potential depredations directed against them and their families and are ready to use force either pre-emptively or in response to both perceived and actual threats. 'Punks', children and women are often defined by either their 'innate' inability to stand up to violence, or by their unwillingness to do so. Such oppositional definitions elicit (or justify) violence against 'punks', while simultaneously curtailing violence against children and women, unless their actions served to remove them symbolically from those protected status positions – something explicitly identified by some respondents.

Chapter 4 focused on how the basic principles of street masculinity were enacted by the men in the sample, especially within the realm of masculinity challenges and violent responses to such challenges. As men engaged each other on the streets, inevitable issues of their own status within the street hierarchy emerged. This jockeying for position took the form of challenges between men who, at their core, played upon the understood expectations and role of violence in interpersonal interactions. I explored how, in various situations, men saw the actions of others as potentially jeopardizing their masculine capital or saw their own actions as potentially increasing said capital. Facing such issues as minor, unintended slights and direct confrontations over money, women and street credibility, the men here were not only cognizant of their masculine reputation, but saw violence as integral to the gendered expectations of themselves and others.

Newburn and Stanko point out that 'all men will not experience or respond to violence in the same way or even in similar ways ... Their experience will be directly mediated by the views of themselves as men, their socially located understanding of what men *are* and the consequences of the experience' (1994: 164, emphasis in original). The findings here can address the relatively underexplored area of men as victims of crime. On the street corner, men who were victimized contextualized the experience in the broader issues of life on the streets – as part and parcel of their daily lives. It was also an experience that required counter-victimization; the masculinity localized on the streets demanded such responses for both ideological and practical reasons. This led men, at least in their discourse, to downplay socio-emotional responses the experience generated (e.g. anxiety, fear, perceived loss of self-control), and to see it simply as a fact of life (further reinforced by the overpowering sense of fatalism with which men interpreted their violent activities). Broader demands of street masculinity led men to interpret victimization not as something that provoked anxiety or fear, but rather as a reputational slight requiring vengeance.

In performing and enacting masculinity on the streets, violence was a common tool – not only for responding to the constant slights and challenges by others, but also for gaining key financial capital to spend in gender-defined ways to further enhance reputation. Armed robbery and carjacking held central positions for many of the men here in obtaining resources for clothes, drugs, cars, women, and other visible signals of street masculinity, while only secondarily being put to use for the more mainstream masculine demands of family support.

Chapter 5 explored the broad scope of the interactions men had with women in their lives – both in the context of their street-corner activities and in the context of their families. This is a severely neglected area in the qualitative study of street crime in general, and the interactions of masculinity with street crime specifically. Much existing feminist criminology has cast such interactions in the light of men's predations on the women they interact with; indeed, the data here described a plethora of such behavior. I hope to have added to these discussions by focusing on these activities from the perspective of the male victimizers. Such a focus is important because it has been relatively underexplored in a streetlife context. The frequent exercise of dominance and control over either women on the streets or those in the men's domestic networks arose out of the demands of street masculinity and the perceptions of women central to it. Streetlife categorized women into a select few categories: objects and family. When interacting with women as objects, men tended to focus their activities on the satisfaction of their sexual and/or criminal desires, using these women to meet broader goals. When interacting with female relatives, be they mothers, grandmothers, sisters, or cousins, many of the men presented themselves in more traditionally defined protective roles. At least in those interactions discussed, the men framed their role in these relationships as protective, insulating the women from the broader dangers of the streets. It is difficult to position wives and steady girlfriends into these dynamics, as they were so infrequently mentioned. While it is never wise to postulate regarding an absence within the data, the absence of romantic partners in the interview could very well suggest that men on the streets who are married or strongly attached to a romantic partner (a rare occurrence here) do not experience an overlap of their domestic relations with their street activities. Such a dynamic was clearly supported by Goldie's brief discussion of his wife in Chapter 5, though this was the only extended discussion of this type.

Additionally, to the extent possible, I have explored the absence of families in the lives of embedded male offenders (see Collier 1998: 20–23). Much of criminology has focused on the connections (or lack thereof) that female offenders have with their families. However, when discussing male criminality researchers have assumed that these ties are absent or unimportant. While this absence may be due to theoretical blind-spots in the conceptualization of the intersections of masculinity and crime; however, it is also due to real interactional vacancies. Further, the lack of evidence concerning men's families is a result of their own alienation from these institutional structures.

Fathers appeared to be absent, and while sisters, mothers and grandmothers were respected and protected, the men spent most of their time away from them and in interactions with other men – thus the extent of family influence may be limited. Family relations are cited as reasons to engage in violence, but there are rare instances when they also deter it. Mothers especially seemed to play a critical role in limiting violence.

Mainstream masculine models as provider and protector were not absent from the mental landscape of the interviewees. Some of the men cited children (or their impending arrival) as motivating forces toward disassociating from the street corner, or at least as a reason to be more cautious in their actions. While men mentioned feeling these pressures, they did not discuss doing much of anything in response. While men did experience this as a contradictory set of behavioral expectations and demands, it was a key point of negotiation. Instead of desistance, they cited being more cautious or careful in their actions, especially when their kids were around. Unfortunately, the samples here were of active offenders and there were no direct questions asked about potential desistance, so I was unable to detect the potential strength of this force. This is one of the key areas that needs more direct inquiry in future research, as many life-course theorists envision parenthood to be a key motivator for potential desistance among both men and women (see Giordano, Cernkovich and Holland 2003; Giordano, Cernkovich and Rudolf 2002; Sampson and Laub 1993).

Chapter 6 explored the many contradictions men had to negotiate in the performance and enactment of street masculinity. Although violence was an almost omnipresent demand, essential disagreements existed over how (and when, and against whom) to accomplish it. One-dimensional demands of toughness, courage, face-building and face-saving pressed men toward frequent, immediate and highly visible displays of combat prowess. Men also gained masculine capital and esteem for possessing 'street smarts', which often dictated that they be less visible in their activities to ensure survival and the avoidance of undue police attention and incarceration. Thus, while there were generally held definitions on the streets that labeled 'sneakiness' (e.g. using surprise as an advantage in carrying out a victimization) as 'punk' behavior, many of the men provided counter-hegemonic definitions of such activities. These emphasized the practicality and security of being sneaky, reframing masculinity to emphasize successful goal accomplishment over rigid adherence to the demands of process. Non-gendered issues of survival and success came into play here: a given man may be forced to sacrifice gender capital to avoid arrest or serious-to-fatal injury. Such a behavioral calculus needs more direct investigation to sort out the influences of gendered versus non-gendered elements.

The most profound set of contradictions emerged in relation to the use of violence against women. In the most general terms, many men claimed not to use violence against women at all in their street-related activities. Making recourse to socialization experiences (e.g. 'My mother taught me never to hit a woman'), references to perceived essentialized differences between the sexes (e.g. 'Women can't take violence like a man can') and bold moral imperatives (e.g. 'It is always wrong to hit a woman'), many men here described inter-gender violence as deviant, even 'punk' behavior. Such denial belies the simple truth that many of these men admitted using violence against women in various contexts. The precise frequency of such violence is difficult to ascertain, as norms of masculinity simultaneously suggest that such behavior is not violence in a street sense and that a man should not advertise engaging in it. When directly confronted with the questions of when, how and why men were violent toward women, a more complex and highly nuanced landscape of violence usage emerged than depicted in the more simplistic denials that violence was ever used against women. While some men still held to the masculinist, even chivalric, view that women simply should not be violently victimized by men, modalities of and rationales for such events rose with frequency as the men engaged in pronounced mental gymnastics to justify their uses of force.

Multiple solutions to this conundrum were presented. One way out of the contradiction was to find other women to exact the violence. A man could save face and reputation, especially if the victimized woman had somehow slighted him, while maintaining a masculine pretense of both protection of women and disinterest in the actions and affairs of women. Alternatively, he could use violence but limit its severity. Since the perceived innate differences between men and women revolved around a woman's lesser capacity to handle violence, a man simply used less force when responding to personal slights and affronts. Others discussed a 'line' crossed by a woman's behavior that allowed her to be classified as a man in terms of violence. Some of the men claimed that by engaging in theft of money or drugs, or by using serious violence herself, a woman abandoned her gender, 'acted like a man', and thus ceded the protections otherwise afforded to her. A rare few indicated that they simply saw no difference between men and women when it came to selecting targets for their violence.

No gendered (or non-gendered) set of behavioral expectations is monolithic; any set of social expectations involves contradictions concerning proper or allowable performance. Social actors negotiate these perceived demands in their gendered actions. Contradictions within street masculinity are moderated by situational elements surrounding the stimulus of and responses to violence. Simply put, while there may be a ubiquitous pressure on men embedded in streetlife to use violence, whether they do so and exactly how they do so will be shaped by the specific situations surrounding either the catalyst of the violence or its execution. My discussions here emphasize the fluid, contradictory nature of street masculinity. Indeed, feminist studies of women's offending have dealt more extensively with these issues; I have tried here to bring some of that complexity to the analysis of men's violence on the streets.

Alienation and the evolution of street masculinity

Street masculinity, as defined and explored here, is a specifically situated constellation of masculine demands and viewpoints that has evolved in the specific context of life within disadvantaged communities. In many ways it is a refraction of broader concerns of maleness; aggressiveness, assertiveness, public face and image, and the domination of other men and women have long been central pillars within western masculinities. Compounded alienations of racial and class-rooted distance from mainstream cultural and structural opportunities establishes a vacuum of social resources to be used in masculinity constructions. The hyper-individuality expressed in the discourses analyzed in Chapter 4 is not simply the rugged individualism of general US (and to a degree western) masculinity, but an intensification of this ideology fueled by the lack of social and other support structures. In many ways, these men truly could only trust and rely upon themselves. Some of this isolation is indeed a product of their own actions and desires – heavy involvement in criminal activities indeed separates the individual from normative social relations. Yet the path toward criminality is enhanced by the lack of mainstream opportunities for prestige and income. The separation is personal, but also cultural, economic, political and geographic. In fact, it is this isolative character that underlies much of street masculinity and must be highlighted to explain its current and historical forms. Since the days of the early Chicago School of sociology, it has been well known that when the standard mechanism of socialization and social control are weak, alternative prestige and behavior structures emerge to fill the gap.

Connell (1993: 602) has suggested that 'masculinity as personal practice cannot be isolated from its institutional context,' it is in fact 'an aspect of institutions' that is (re)produced in interpersonal actions and lifeways. As with all social life, key institutions frame social dynamics; for understanding masculinities, Connell (1993) draws our attention specifically to the state, the workplace/labor market, and the family. The centrality of these loci of power and its exercise within any society is undeniable; the base impotence of these institutional arrangements within the lives of the men explored here is similarly undeniable. Street masculinity is a situated rejection of and strong resistance to the more generally advocated expressions of manhood in the US. Yet, as shown, it is not a wholesale rejection of core ideas and images, but an attempt to reshape and redefine masculinity based upon the resources that are available and usable within the context of streetlife social networks.

Throughout the analysis here, the men whose lives have been the subject of study have repeatedly been characterized by their disconnection from mainstream social life. The only experiences of the state come from frequent and hostile contact with the local police. The conditions of post-industrial labor markets, and their own behaviors, isolated them from the legal economy. Family connections were tenuous and problematic at best. The notion that manhood can be constructed from citizenship, legal labor and heading a household were not alien concepts to these men's worldviews or lives; workable models of such mainstream masculinity were visible in their own neighborhoods as well as ubiquitously presented in the media and other loci of socialization. Yet the habitus of streetlife rejects and condemns these lives as out of reach and lacking in meaning.

It is in the absence of these identity-generating social loci that violence, sexual conquest and flossing become almost the be all and end all of reputation construction and maintenance. In dialectical fashion, this enactment of street masculinity increases the alienation and dislocation experienced by the men who turn toward it for a sense of being and place. These processes codify and crystallize both a criminal and street-based masculine identity that is self-reinforcing and internally intensifying.

It is within these macro and meso level conditions that men made their decisions about violence. As shown throughout the volume, even the most violent men here were not always violent. Often, it was enough to have a reputation of toughness and power. In entering into any social interaction, the men had to decide whether or not to be violent, and if so, the degree of severity to enact. Who was involved, who was present, the history of interactions, the nature of the current interaction, as well as highly variable issues such as mood, immediately prior experiences, drug and alcohol use (or lack thereof) all set the social context of street violence.

Conclusion

Scholars should be cognizant of the potential to over-ascribe gendered meanings to behaviors that may either be less influenced by gender or non-gendered in their nature (see Miller 2002). Especially when one is using more static, monolithic or essentialized conceptualizations of gender, the danger of applying gender to all aspects of behavior submerges difference, nuance and agency. However, I do not suggest that in order to interpret behavior as gendered, the subjects must emphasize or explicitly verbalize the behavior as such. It is the distinct privilege of social theorists, especially those working at the macro level, to frame and explore causal forces of social behavior that go unrecognized by social actors themselves. It is the purview of broader feminist theory construction to identify what is, what may be, and what is not gendered – and then apply such frameworks to the actions and narratives of individuals. This is the essential nature of etic theorization – even when using emic-oriented data to build such theory.

In making these theoretical claims, it is not my intent to deny social actors a sense of agency or to suggest that scholars reduce their focus on the role that agency plays within offending behaviors. In fact, the contradictions that emerged in the data are excellent examples of how agentic decision-making shapes violence, especially inter-gender violence, on the streets of Saint Louis. While violence can be stimulated and structured by gender, these demands are not monolithic. Contrary demands of masculinity or other, more distinctly practical, considerations (e.g. survival) can moderate broader pushes toward violence. Gender is clearly one of the many structural and situational elements that bound the rationality at work here.

In this volume I have brought current trends in feminist criminological theory and research to bear on our understanding of the interconnections between masculinity and violence. Too often in criminology, the 'gender problem' is simply taken for granted – the dominance of men among the ranks of criminal offenders is assumed. When gender *is* examined, it is too frequently reduced to a dichotomous predictor variable in regression equations to account for a particular amount of variance in the model. Typically little is made of that variance when findings are discussed. Qualitative researchers, especially those working within or sympathetic to feminist theory, have done more in uncovering and unpacking the meanings of gender's influence on offending. Yet more often than not the focus is on women and their experiences as victims and offenders. Men and masculinity are left undertheorized. When attempting to ascertain the role of masculinities within the etiology of offending, such perspectives give little guidance.

In the feminist-inspired research that takes the causal role of masculinities seriously in the study of men's offending, the tendency has been to treat gender as monolithic, omnipresent and almost clumsily causal in nature. Such activities are masculine because men do them and men do them because they are masculine. While this view has been logically critiqued by some as tautological (e.g. Collier 1998), more careful and nuanced understanding of the interactions of social actors within gendered social structures not only diffuses the apparent logical circularity – showing us that individuals and social structure exist in a dialectical relationship of influence – but also guides us to more intricate analyses of the nature of gender and its influence on behavior.

Multiple masculinities exist in western social structures, many drawing to varying degrees on the appearance and use of violence. We must be able to ascertain how and why men activate violence in certain situations and not in others; we must also be able to see the full landscape of agentic choices presented to male actors in regard to violence and how men interpret those variant opportunities in order to understand fully the linkages of masculinity and violence. That has been the focus and contribution of the current investigation.

Notes

1   Another form of masculinity, which only appeared tangentially in the data, was that of the 'straight' man who was not engaged in street or criminal activities. This category only emerged when the men were talking about engaging in legitimate work (something rare here) or in making very broad statements about future aspirations for themselves or their children. This masculinity was difficult to fully describe based on its infrequent discussion. At most, it seems that the men knew it was 'out

there somewhere' in society, but did not engage it on a daily basis and thus it did not take a central role in the definition of a street masculinity identity.

2 The only real difference between the two was number of hours per week/number of weeks per month spent in legitimate (as opposed to illegitimate) work. At the time of the interview, only two of the respondents could be classified as working class – holding full-time jobs that paid above a living wage.

Appendix

Master sample list

Street name	Sample	Age	Sex
Darnell	Drug robber	25	Male
Curly	Drug robber	45	Male
Ray Dog	Drug robber	40	Male
Lewis	Drug robber	36	Male
Slim	Drug robber	46	Male
Spanky	Drug robber	20	Male
Blackwell	Drug robber	34	Male
YoYo	Drug robber	27	Female
Ladybug	Drug robber	30	Female
Do Dirty	Drug robber	39	Male
Baby Doll	Drug robber	38	Female
Lowdown	Drug robber	32	Male
Three-Eye	Drug robber	25	Male
Kilo	Drug robber	25	Male
Buck	Drug robber	40	Male
Junebug	Drug robber	44	Male
Crazy Jack	Drug robber	17	Male
Snap	Drug robber	26	Male
Lil' Player	Drug robber	15	Male
Looney Ass Nigger	Drug robber	19	Male
Bacca	Drug robber	19	Male
J-Rock	Drug robber	39	Male
Jay	Drug robber	39	Male
Smooth G	Drug robber	19	Female

Street name	Sample	Age	Sex
K-Red	Drug robber	17	Male
Ray Ray	Drug robber	19	Male
Big Mix	Carjacker	22	Female
C-Ball	Carjacker	20	Male
Low	Carjacker	33	Male
Nicole	Carjacker	22	Female
C-Low	Carjacker	22	Male
Popo	Carjacker	35	Female
Sexy Diva	Carjacker	28	Female
Binge	Carjacker	45	Male
Little Tye	Carjacker	19	Male
Little Rag	Carjacker	19	Male
Loco	Carjacker	20	Male
Mo	Carjacker	23	Male
Playboy	Carjacker	19	Male
Tall	Carjacker	37	Male
Snake	Carjacker	18	Male
Beano	Snitch	25	Male
Big Mix 2	Snitch	41	Female
Cal	Snitch	22	Male
Cora	Snitch	24	Male
J	Snitch	26	Male
Jack-T	Snitch	52	Male
K-Ill	Snitch	23	Male
Nasty Bitch	Snitch	29	Female
Neck	Snitch	40	Male
Peaches	Snitch	23	Female
Pie	Snitch	26	Male
Rock	Snitch	20	Male
Sleazy-E	Snitch	30	Male
Smokedog (2)	Snitch	42	Male
Stacy	Snitch	18	Female
W.Florissant	Snitch	24	Male
Hodemont	Retaliation	26	Female
Biddle	Retaliation	28	Male
Big C	Retaliation	50	Male
Big Mac	Retaliation	29	Male
Big Will	Retaliation	31	Male
Bishop	Retaliation	32	Male
Black1	Retaliation	26	Male

Street name	Sample	Age	Sex
Noir (Black2)	Retaliation	24	Male
Bobcat	Retaliation	18	Male
Chewy	Retaliation	16	Male
Duff	Retaliation	45	Male
CrazyJay	Retaliation	20	Male
D-Boy	Retaliation	26	Male
TD	Retaliation	18	Male
Speezy	Retaliation	25	Male
DL	Retaliation	38	Male
Don Love	Retaliation	24	Male
Hops	Retaliation	25	Male
Icy Mike	Retaliation	27	Male
Frizz	Retaliation	59	Female
Jhustle	Retaliation	23	Male
Jaymoon	Retaliation	25	Male
Jay	Retaliation	21	Male
Kimmy	Retaliation	21	Female
K-LOC	Retaliation	26	Female
Lady Ice	Retaliation	27	Female
Lafonz	Retaliation	25	Male
Mad Dog	Retaliation	20	Male
Miss Dee	Retaliation	24	Female
Moon	Retaliation	27	Male
Paris	Retaliation	44	Male
Player	Retaliation	28	Male
Geasy	Retaliation	21	Male
Gerry	Retaliation	32	Male
Dub	Retaliation	18	Male
Big D	Retaliation	33	Female
Play Too Much	Retaliation	24	Male
Pooh Bear	Retaliation	24	Female
Red	Retaliation	43	Male
TC	Retaliation	26	Male
TDog	Retaliation	23	Male
Sheryl	Retaliation	18	Female
T-Dog	Retaliation	23	Male
Teaser	Retaliation	33	Female
E	Retaliation	37	Male
Goldie	Multiple	27	Male
Smokedog	Multiple	22	Male

Street name	Sample	Age	Sex
V-0	Multiple	29	Male
Kow	Multiple	24	Male
Block	Multiple	22	Male
Pumpkin	Multiple	21	Female
Sugar	Multiple	No data	Female
Sleezee-E	Multiple	33	Male

References

Adler, Christine and Kenneth Polk, 1996, 'Masculinity and Child Homicide', *British Journal of Criminology*, 36(3): 396–411.

Akerstrom, Malin, 1985, *Crooks and Squares*. New Brunswick, NJ: Transaction.

Anderson, Elijah, 1999, *Code of the Street: Decency, Violence and the Moral Life of the Inner City*. New York: W. W. Norton.

—— 1990, *Streetwise: Race, Class and Change in an Urban Community*. Chicago: University of Chicago Press.

Bailey, F. Y. and A. P. Green, 1999, *Law Never Here: A Social History of African American Responses to Issues of Crime and Justice*. Westport, CT: Praeger.

Babbie, Earl, 1998, *The Practice of Social Research*. 8th edition. Belmont, CA: Wadsworth ITP.

Beiser, Vincent, 2005, 'A Guilty Man', *Mother Jones*, September/October: 34–9.

Bourgois, Philippe, 1996, 'In Search of Masculinity: Violence, Respect and Sexuality among Puerto Rican Crack Dealers in East Harlem', *British Journal of Criminology*, 36: 412–27.

—— 1995, *In Search of Respect: Selling Crack in El Barrio*. Cambridge, UK: Cambridge University Press.

Campbell, Anne, 1999, 'Female Gang Member's Social Representations of Aggression', in Meda Chesney-Lind and John H. Hagedorn (eds), *Female Gangs in America*. Chicago: Lakeview Press: 248–55.

Cernkovich, Stephen A., 1978, 'Value Orientations and Delinquency Involvement', *Criminology* 15: 443–58.

Chesney-Lind, Meda, 1997, *The Female Offender: Girls, Women and Crime*. Thousand Oaks, CA: Sage.

Cohen, Albert, 1955, *Delinquent Boys*. New York: Free Press.

Collier, Richard, 1998, *Masculinities, Crime and Criminology: Men, Heterosexuality and the Criminal(ised) Other*. London: Sage.

Collison, Mike, 1996, 'In Search of the High Life: Drugs, Crime, Masculinities and Consumption', *British Journal of Criminology*, 36: 428–44.

Connell, R. W., 2002, *Gender*. Cambridge, UK: Polity Press.

—— 1995, *Masculinities*. Berkeley, CA: University of California Press.

—— 1993, 'The Big Picture: Masculinites in Recent World History', *Theory and Society*, 22: 597–623.

—— 1987, *Gender and Power: Society, the Person and Sexual Politics*. Stanford, CA: Stanford University Press.

Connell, R. W. and James Messerschmidt, 2005, 'Hegemonic Masculinity: Rethinking the Concept. *Gender and Society*, 19(6): 829–59.

Corti, Louise, Janet Foster and Paul Thompson, 1995, 'Archiving Qualitative Research Data', *Social Research Update*, 10.

Daly, Kathleen, 1997, 'Different Ways of Conceptualizing Sex/Gender in Feminist Theory and their Implications for Criminology', *Theoretical Criminology*. 1(1): 25–51.

Davidson, R. Theodore, 1974, *Chicano Prisoners: The Key to San Quentin*. Prospect Heights, IL: Waveland.

Decker, Scott H. and Barrik Van Winkle, 1996, *Life in the Gang*. Cambridge, UK: Cambridge University Press.

Federal Bureau of Investigation, 2002, *Crime in the United States: 2001*. Washington D.C.: Department of Justice.

Freud, Sigmund, 1924, *A General Introduction to Psychoanalysis*. New York: Boni and Liveright.

Garfinkel, Harold, 1967, *Studies in Ethnomethodology*. Englewood Cliffs, NJ: Prentice Hall.

Gilbert, Dennis, 1998, *The American Class Structure in an Age of Growing Inequality*, 5th edition. Belmont, CA: Wadsworth.

Giordano, Peggy, Stephen A. Cernkovich and Donna D. Holland, 2003, 'Changes in Friendship Relations over the Life Course: Implications for Desistance from Crime', *Criminology* 41(2): 293–327.

Giordano, Peggy, Stephen A. Cernkovich and Jennifer Rudolf, 2002, 'Gender, Crime and Desistance: Toward a Theory of Cognitive Transformation', *American Journal of Sociology*, 107(4): 990–1064.

Goffman, Erving, 1983, 'The Interaction Order: American Sociological Association, 1982 Presidential address', *American Sociological Review* 48(1): 1–17.

—— 1959, *The Presentation of Self in Everyday Life*. Garden City, NY: Doubleday.

—— 1955, *Interaction Ritual: Essays on Face to Face Behavior*. Garden City, NY: Anchor.

Goode, William J., 1960, 'A theory of role strain', *American Sociological Review*, 25: 483–96.

Graham, Kathryn and Samantha Wells, 2003, '"Somebody's gonna get their head kicked in tonight!": Aggression Among Young Males in Bars – A Question of Values?' *British Journal of Criminology*, 43(3): 546–66.

Gramsci, Antonio, 1992, *Prison Notebooks*. New York: Columbia University Press.

Hagan, John and Bill McCarthy, 1997, *Mean Streets: Youth Crime and Homelessness*. Cambridge, UK: Cambridge University Press.

Heaton, Janet, 1998, 'Secondary Analysis of Qualitative Data', *Social Research Update*, 22.

Hinds, Pamela S., Ralph J. Vogal and Laura Clarke–Steffen, 1997, 'The Possibilities and Pitfalls of doing Secondary Analysis of a Qualitative Data Set', *Qualitative Health Research*, 7(3): 408–24.

Hirschi, Travis, 1969, *Causes of Delinquency*. Berkeley, CA: University of California Press.

Hobbs, Dick, 1994, 'Mannish Boys: Danny, Chris, Crime, Masculinity and Business', in Tim Newburn and Elizabeth Stanko (eds), *Just Boys Doing Business? Men, Masculinities and Crime*. London: Routledge: 118–34.

Hobbs, Dick, Philip Hadfield, Stuart Lister and Simon Winlow, 2003, *Bouncers: Violence and Governance in the Night-time Economy*. Oxford, UK: Oxford University Press.

Irwin, John, 1980, *Prisons in Turmoil*. Boston: Little, Brown and Company.

Jacobs, Bruce A., 2000, *Robbing Drug Dealers: Violence Beyond the Law*. New York: Aldine de Gruyter.

—— 1999, *Dealing Crack: The Social World of Streetcorner Selling*. Boston, MA: Northeastern University Press.

Jacobs, Bruce A. and Jody A. Miller, 1998, 'Crack Dealing, Gender and Arrest Avoidance', *Social Problems* 45(4): 550–69.

Jacobs, Bruce A., Volkan Topalli and Richard T. Wright, 2000, 'Managing Retaliation: Drug Robbery and Informal Sanction Threats', *Criminology*, 38(1): 171–98.

Jankowski, Martin Sanchez, 1991, *Island in the Street: Gangs and American Urban Society*. Berkeley, CA: University of California Press.

Katz, Jack, 1988, *Seductions of Crime: A Chilling Exploration of the Criminal Mind – From Juvenile Delinquency to Cold-Blooded Murder*. New York: Basic Books.

Kimmel, Michael, 2005, 'Globalization and its Mal(e)Contents: The Gendered Moral and Political Economy of Terrorism', in M. S. Kimmel, J. Hearn and R. W. Connell (eds), *Handbook of Studies on Men and Masculinities*. Thousand Oaks, CA: Sage.

—— 1996, *Manhood in America: A Cultural History*. New York: The Free Press.

Kupers, Terry A., 2001, Rape and the Prison Code', D. Sabo, T. Kupers and W. London (eds), *Prison Masculinities*. Philadelphia, PA: Temple University Press: 111–17.

Laub, John H., Daniel S. Nagin and Robert J. Sampson, 1998, 'Trajectories of Change in Criminal Offending: Good Marriages and the Desistance Process', *American Sociological Review*, 63: 225–38.

MacLeod, Jay, 1995, *Ain't No Makin' It: Aspirations and Attainment in a Low-Income Neighborhood*. Boulder, CO: Westview.

Maher, Lisa, 1997, *Sexed Work: Gender, Race and Resistance in a Brooklyn Drug Market*. Oxford, UK: Oxford University Press.

Majors, Richard and Janet Mancini Billson, 1993, *Cool Pose: The Dilemmas of Black Manhood in America*. New York: Touchstone.

Maruna, Shadd, 2001, *Making Good: How Ex-Convicts Reform and Rebuild Their Lives*. Washington D.C.: American Psychological Association.

Massey, Douglas S. and Nancy Denton, 1993, *American Apartheid: Segregation and the Making of the Underclass*. Cambridge, MA: Harvard University Press.

McAdams, Dan, 2001, *Coding Autobiographical Episodes for Themes of Agency and Communion*. Evanston, IL: Foley Center for the Study of Lives, Northwestern University.

—— 1993, *The Stories We Live By: Personal Myths and the Making of the Self*. New York: William Morrow.

Merton, Robert, 1938, 'Social Structure and Anomie', *American Sociological Review*, 3(6): 672–82.

Messerschmidt, James W., 2004, *Flesh and Blood: Adolescent Gender Diversity and Violence*. Lanham: Rowman and Littlefield.

—— 2000, *Nine Lives: Adolescent Masculinities, the Body, and Violence*. Boulder, CO: Westview.

—— 1997, *Crime as Structured Action: Gender, Race, Class and Crime in the Making*. Thousand Oaks, CA: Sage.

—— 1993, *Masculinities and Crime: Critique and Reconceptualization of Theory*. Lanham, MD: Rowan and Little Field.

Miller, Jody, 2002, 'The Strengths and Limits of "Doing Gender" for Understanding Street Crime', *Theoretical Criminology*, 6: 433–60.

—— 2001, *One of the Guys: Girls, Gangs and Gender*. New York: Oxford University Press.

—— 1998, 'Up it Up: Gender and the Accomplishment of Street Robbery', *Criminology*, 36: 37–66.

Miller, Jody and Christopher W. Mullins, 2006a, 'Stuck up, Telling Lies and Talking Too Much: The Gendered Context of Young Women's Violence', in Karen Heimer and Candace Kruttschmidt (eds), *New Directions in the*

Study of Gender, Crime and Victimization. New York: Routledge: 41–66.

—— 2006b, 'Taking Stock: The Status of Feminist Theories in Criminology', in Francis Cullen, John Paul Wright and Kristie Blevins (eds), *Taking Stock: The Status of Criminological Theory, Advances in Criminological Theory*, Vol. 15, New Jersey: Transaction Publishers.

Miller, Jody and Norman A. White, 2003, 'Gender and Adolescent Relationship Violence: A Contextual Examination', *Criminology*, 41(4): 1501–41.

Miller, Walter, 1958, 'Lower Class Culture as a Generating Milieu of Gang Delinquency', *Journal of Social Issues*, 14: 5–19.

Montgomery, Heather, 2001, *Modern Babylon? Prostituting Children in Thailand*. New York: Berghahn Books.

Mullins, Christopher W., 2006, 'Women and Violence on the Streets: Resistance and Empowerment in Streetlife Social Networks', in Tammy Anderson (ed.), *Women, Power and Drugs*. Piscataway, NJ: Rutger's University Press.

Mullins, Christopher W. and Richard T. Wright, 2003, 'Gender, Social Networks and Residential Burglary', *Criminology* 41(3): 813–40.

Mullins, Christopher W., Richard T. Wright and Bruce A. Jacobs, 2004, 'Gender, Streetlife and Criminal Retaliation', *Criminology* 42(4): 911–40.

Newburn, Tim and Elizabeth Stanko, 1994, *Just Boys Doing Business? Men, Masculinities and Crime*. London: Routledge.

Nurse, Anne M., 2002, 'The Structure of the Juvenile Prison: Constructing the Inmate Father', *Youth and Society*, 32(3): 368–99.

Oliver, William, 1994, *The Violent Social World of Black Men*. New York: Lexington Books.

Orbuch, Terri L., 1997, 'People's Accounts Count: The Sociology of Accounts', *Annual Review of Sociology*, 23: 455–78.

Parsons, Talcott, 1955, 'The American Family: Its Relations to Personality and to the Social Structure', in Talcott Parson and Robert Bales (eds), *Family, Socialization and Interaction Processes*, Glenco, IL: Free Press: 3–33.

Polk, Kenneth, 1994, 'Masculinity, Honor and Confrontational Homicide', in Tim Newburn and Elizabeth Stanko (eds), *Just Boys Doing Business? Men, Masculinities and Crime*. London: Routledge: 166–88.

Pollak, Otto, 1950, *The Criminality of Women*. Philadelphia: University of Pennsylvania Press.

Riedel, Marc and Wayne Welsh, 2002, *Criminal Violence: Patterns, Causes and Prevention*. Los Angeles, CA: Roxbury.

Rosenfeld, Richard, Bruce A. Jacobs and Richard T. Wright, 2003, 'Snitching and the Code of the Street', *British Journal of Criminology*, 43: 291–309.

Roy, William G., 2001, *Making Societies*. Thousand Oaks, CA: Pine Forge Press.

Sampson, Robert J. and Dawn J. Bartusch, 1999, *Attitudes Toward Crime, Police and the Law: Individual and Neighborhood Differences*. Washington D.C.: Department of Justice, National Institute of Justice.

Sampson, Robert and John Laub, 1993, *Crime in the Making: Pathways and Turning Points Through Life*. Cambridge, MA: Harvard University Press.

Santacroce, Sheila J., Janet A. Deatrick and Susan W. Ledlie, 2000, 'Secondary Analysis of Qualitative Data: A Means of Collaborations in HIV-related Research', *Journal of the Association of Nurses in AIDS Care*, 11(3): 99–104.

Scully, Diana, 1990, *Understanding Sexual Violence: A Study of Convicted Rapists*. New York: Routledge.

Sellin, Thorsten, 1938, *Culture Conflict and Crime*. New York: Social Science Research Council.

Shannon, Lyle, 1988, *Criminal Career Continuity: Its Social Context*. New York: Human Sciences Press.

Shover, Neal, 1996, *Great Pretenders: Pursuits and Careers of Persistent Thieves*. Boulder, CO: Westview.

Shover, Neal and Belinda Henderson, 1995, 'Repressive Crime Control and Male Persistent Thieves', in H. Barlow (ed.), *Crime and Public Policy: Putting Theory to Work*. Boulder, CO: Westview.

Shover, Neal and David Honaker, 1992, 'The Socially Bounded Decision Making of Persistent Property Offenders', *Howard Journal of Criminal Justice* 31: 276–93.

Sim, Joe, 1994, 'Tougher Than the Rest? Men in Prison', in Tim Newburn and Elizabeth Stanko (eds), *Just Boys Doing Business? Men, Masculinities and Crime*. London: Routledge: 100–17.

Simpson, Sally, 1991, 'Caste, Class, and Violent Crime: Explaining Difference in Female Offending', *Criminology*, 29: 115–35.

Simpson, Sally and Lori Elis, 1995, 'Doing Gender: Sorting Out the Caste and Crime Conundrum', *Criminology* 33: 47–81.

Spradley, James, 1979, *The Ethnographic Interview*. Orlando, Florida: Holt, Rinehart, Winston.

Staples, Robert, 1982, *Black Masculinity: The Black Male's Role in American Society*. San Francisco: Black Scholar Press.

Steffensmeier, Darrell, 1983, 'Organization Properties and Sex-segregation in the Underworld: Building a Sociological Theory of Sex Differences in Crime', *Social Forces*, 61: 1010–32.

Steffensmeier, Darrell and Robert Terry, 1986, 'Institutional Sexism in the Underworld: A View from the Inside', *Sociological Inquiry*, 56: 304–23.

Suarez, Ray, 1999, *The Old Neighborhood: What We Lost in the Great Suburban Migration, 1966–1999*. New York: Free Press.

Sutherland, E., 1939, 'White Collar Criminality', *American Sociological Review*, 5: 1–12.

Sykes, Gresham M. and David Matza, 1957, 'Techniques of Neutralization: A Theory of Delinquency', *American Sociological Review*, 22: 664–70.

Thorne, Sally, 1998, 'Ethical and Representational Issues in Qualitative Secondary Analysis', *Qualitative Health Research*, 8(4): 547–55.

Tomsen, Stephen, 1997, 'A Top Night: Social Protest, Masculinity and the Culture of Drinking Violence', *British Journal of Criminology*, 37(1): 90–102.

Topalli, Volkan, 2005, 'When Being Good is Bad: An Expansion of Neutralization Theory', *Criminology*, 43(3): 797–835.

Topalli, Volkan, Richard T. Wright and Robert Fornango, 2002, 'Drug Dealers, Robbery and Retaliation: Vulnerability, Deterrence, and the Contagion of Violence', *The British Journal of Criminology*, 42(2): 337–51.

Tunnel, Kenneth, 2000, *Living Off Crime*. Chicago: Burnham.

—— 1992, *Choosing Crime: The Criminal Calculus of Property Offenders*. Chicago: Nelson-Hall.

United States Census Bureau, 2000, *Population and Housing Profile: St. Louis City. Census 2000 Supplementary Survey*. Washington D.C.: US Census Bureau.

Visher, Christy A., 2000, 'Career Criminals and Crime Control', in Joseph F. Sheley (ed.), *Criminology: A Contemporary Handbook*. Belmont, CA: Wadsworth: 601–19.

Warr, Mark, 2002, *Companions in Crime: The Social Aspects of Criminal Conduct*. Cambridge: Cambridge University Press.

—— 1998, 'Life-course Transitions and Desistance from Crime', *Criminology*, 36(1): 183–216.

—— 1996, 'Organization and Instigation in Delinquent Groups', *Criminology*, 34(1): 11–37.

Weller, Susan and A. Kimball Romney, 1988, *Systematic Data Collection. Qualitative Research Methods Series*, Volume 10. Thousand Oaks, CA: Sage.

West, Candace and Sarah Fenstermaker, 1995, 'Doing Difference', *Gender and Society*, 9: 3–37.

West, Candace and Don Zimmerman, 1987, 'Doing Gender', *Gender and Society*, 1: 125–51.

Williams, John and Rogan Taylor, 1994, 'Boys Keep Swinging: Masculinity and Football Culture in England', in Tim Newburn and Elizabeth Stanko (eds.), *Just Boys Doing Business? Men, Masculinities and Crime*. London: Routledge: 214–33.

Willis, Paul, 1977, *Learning to Labor*. Aldershot: Gower.

Wilson, William J., 1987, *The Truly Disadvantaged: The Inner City, The Underclass and Public Policy*. Chicago: University of Chicago Press.

—— 1996, *When Work Disappears: The World of the New Urban Poor*. New York: Alfred A. Knopf.

Winlow, Simon, 2001, *Badfellas: Crime, Tradition and New Masculinities*. Oxford: Berg.

Wolfgang, Marvin E. and Franco Ferracuti, 1967, *The Subculture of Violence*. London: Tavistock.

Wolfgang, Marvin E., Robert M. Figlio and Thorsten Sellin, 1972, *Delinquency in a Birth Cohort*. Chicago: University of Chicago Press.

Wright, Richard, Scott Decker, Allison Redfern and Dietrich Smith, 1992, 'A Snowball's Chance in Hell: Doing Fieldwork with Active Residential Burglars', *Journal of Research in Crime and Delinquency*, 29: 148–61.

Wright, Richard and Scott Decker, 1994, *Burglars on the Job: Streetlife and Residential Break-ins*. Boston: Northeastern University Press.

—— 1997, *Armed Robbers in Action: Stick Ups and Street Culture*. Boston: Northeastern University Press.

Index

abuse, of jacked cars 72
acquaintances, as source of danger 55
acquisitive crimes 15, 17, 21, 63
African-Americans
    use of violence 24–5
    vigilante justice 123–4
age
    changing attitudes 54
    independence 52
    street hierarchies 81
alcohol, and violence 84
alienation 14, 74, 158–60
anomie theory 11
anti-police attitudes 100–1
appearance 18, 71
armed robbery 15, 21, 61, 65, 154
aspirations 61, 75, 123
assaults, fatal 18
attitudes
    lower-class community 3, 11, 12
    of women towards men 116
    see also negative attitudes

Bacca 51, 55, 58, 62, 71, 88, 109, 116–17, 121
bars, incidents of violence 84
Beano 53, 100

behavioural demands
    negotiation of contradictory 156
    oppositional resistance to mainstream 3
    street masculinity 18
    streetlife 4
behavioural expectations 9, 11, 74, 155
behaviours
    differing standards for judging 128
    gendered 5–6
    punk (subordinate masculinity) 63, 128, 147
'being talked down to' 87–91
Biddle 78, 92
Big C 58, 101
Big Mac 135–6, 142, 143
Big Mix 55, 58, 111
Big Will 67, 101, 116
Binge 70, 72
Bishop 119–20, 122, 123–4, 126n
Black 51, 52, 67, 79–80, 92, 96, 117, 128–9, 132, 133
black street masculinity 24–5
Blackwell 121
Block 54–5, 98, 107
bouncers 17